THE OTHER SIDE OF
LEADERSHIP

The Other Side Of Leadership

EUGENE B. HABECKER

VICTOR BOOKS ®

A DIVISION OF SCRIPTURE PRESS PUBLICATIONS INC.
USA CANADA ENGLAND

Unless otherwise indicated, all Scripture quotations are from the *Holy Bible, New International Version,* © 1973, 1978, 1984, International Bible Society. Used by permission of Zondervan Bible Publishers. Others are from the *King James Version* (KJV) and *The Living Bible* (TLB), © 1971, Tyndale House Publishers, Wheaton, IL 60189. Used by permission.

Cover Photo: Comstock

Recommended Dewey Decimal Classification: 658
Suggested Subject Heading: LEADERSHIP

Library of Congress Catalog Card Number: 87-81023
ISBN: 0-89693-341-5   BV 652, H3

VICTOR BOOKS
A division of SP Publications, Inc.
Wheaton, Illinois 60187

C O N T E N T S

To Marylou, my best friend and the love of my life,
and to our three special
children—David, Matthew,
and Marybeth.
Together, they are my encouragers
in leading and following.

ACKNOWLEDGMENTS

A book such as this could not be written without the efforts and practical examples and models of others. Many come to mind. Several are mentioned. Orville and Ruth Merillat, founders of Merillat Industries, have demonstrated these principles of leading and following in the corporate business world. John Dellenback, president of the Christian College Coalition and former member of Congress and head of the Peace Corps, has demonstrated these concepts in the world of education and government. The Board of Trustees of Huntington College, along with its faculty and staff, have been my colleagues and co-laborers as we together work out these leading/following ideas and considerations.

Special mention must be made of Greg Clouse, my editor at Victor Books. As expected, he provided many helpful and useful suggestions and additions. Additionally, I must mention the graciousness of President and Mrs. Joe Hagen of Assumption College. Their hospitality made possible significant work on the manuscript during several weeks of the summer of 1986. Finally, I want to express special appreciation to my administrative assistant, Beth Lahr. She expertly and patiently supervised the preparation of the manuscript.

FOREWORD

Every organization has its leaders.

Some are self-selected. Some are elected or otherwise chosen by the organization. Some are appointed by higher levels of leadership.

Some arise or appear in times of crisis, and when the crises are gone, so also are the leaders. Others exercise leadership over long periods of time, in times of difficulty and in times of tranquility, and the leadership ends only when their lives do.

Some leaders have very evident trappings of power and authority. Others function without such trappings clearly seen or even present.

Some leadership power and authority are very limited in scope. The power and authority of other leaders seem open-ended.

Some leaders follow one style of leadership. Others lead in a very different way. Some styles of leadership seem to work well in certain situations and not in others. Some styles are for all seasons.

Some persons become leaders of existing organizations. Others are leaders in thought and action, trailblazers who gradually attract others to follow where once they thought and walked alone.

Some observers feel that leaders are born, not made. Other observers or even participants feel that leadership is teachable and that at least most people can become leaders. That is to a degree an underlying premise of this book.

Dr. Gene Habecker moves into this confused and confusing situation with some clear and helpful thinking. He expresses his intention of laying out his ideas and thoughts as a good beginning, not as the final word on the subject.

Dr. Habecker's own track record is that of a leader. Having earned both a Ph.D. and a J.D., he has served effectively within the educational hierarchy as a college dean of students, executive vice president, and president. He has also served outside the formal educational hierarchy in a variety of leadership positions.

One need be around him only a short while to become keenly aware of his constant spinning off of ideas and his leading out with provocative thoughts and concepts. His record demonstrates clearly the characteristic operational style of transforming ideas into action, of drawing others into following those ideas with him, and of his often being chosen to lead.

In this book Dr. Habecker investigates the leadership traits of a number of Old Testament greats. He observes and analyzes how these revered leaders dealt with some of the obvious challenges of leadership as well as with the so often unseen challenges that arise from human nature. Therein lie some clear lessons for us in the modern world.

Admittedly the biblical account often lacks details we would find valuable in seeking guidance for dealing with many of today's intensely practical problems. But Gene Habecker seeks to extract principles and lessons from what we *do* find and then to apply them to various aspects of this important subject of leadership.

The subject is important. The source upon which the author draws is the best. The observations and reasoning are thought-provoking and sound. The applications and suggestions are valuable and frequent. The book is well worth reading.

John R. Dellenback
President
Christian College Coalition

INTRODUCTION

According to a recent newspaper article dealing with the subject of leaders, power, and religious sects, "Americans are flocking to new ... Christian sects dominated by leaders who exercise virtually unlimited control over members' lives and thoughts.... What sets the new groups apart ... is the great degree of power held by the leaders."[1] According to another commentator, "Leadership is a legitimate area of ... inquiry that is little examined."[2]

Increasing numbers of advertisements appear in Christian publications announcing leadership clinics and workshops. Christian organizations, including churches, pursue their quest for solid leadership. Christian colleges boldly announce programs for student leaders and diligently seek to attract students who want to be leaders. Alternatively, few colleges or other Christian organizations are attempting to recruit those who wish to be followers. Leadership is "in" and followership is "out"—at least judging by the absence of advertisements for followership clinics.

In part, this call for renewed emphasis on leadership is related to the fact that many Christian organizations are struggling financially (a condition presumably not desired by God and something good leadership would correct), and also because available resources and technology are not properly harnessed to effect the implementation and achievement of kingdom priorities.

This book is addressed to those who desire to be leaders— persons who believe they can and must make a difference in their church, their organization, their families, and their communities. This broad application to a wide variety of persons and settings reflects my thinking, at least in part, of the definition of a leader— someone who dares to make a difference in a given sphere of influence and who is committed to do so following biblical principles.

This book is not intended to be the final word on the subject of leadership. Rather, it represents what is hoped will be a good beginning. In that context, this book has relevance for those who consider themselves to be leaders. There are few persons indeed who do not have the capacity to make a difference where God has placed them. In particular, however, this book is intended to be a kind of primer on leadership for those people who, in addition to the chief executive officer (CEO) or pastor, lead in the context of the Christian organization. Literally thousands of people find themselves in these kinds of roles.

While a variety of secular sources speak to the issue of leadership—and many will be referred to in this volume—particular attention will be given to the living examples of leadership presented in Scripture. It's one thing to talk about leadership in a vacuum, distilling a variety of dicta reflecting personal bias in support of leadership perceptions. It's quite another to look at the actual performance of leaders not chosen by the board or by the people of the organization, but rather by God, and to see how they performed and what qualities they possessed. In particular, then, frequent reference will be made to the leadership examples of Moses, Joshua, David, and others. Further, a particular focus of this book will be to look not only at the public or visible side of the leader but also to look at the more private side—the other side of the leader. The focus will be both organizational (how, for example, the leader deals with organizational issues such as following, trusting, confronting, and forgiving) and personal (how, for example, the leader deals with issues such as family, salary, sexuality, and vulnerability). The focus will address accountability with regard to both God and the people being led.

The book is divided into three parts. The first part reviews basic concepts of leadership (including those of power and authority) as expressed in a wide variety of literature. The intent for doing this is to provide an operative context for leadership so that, as we proceed, we will have a common understanding of terms and concepts.

The second part will focus on what I call the organizational dimension of leadership—that is, the leader's responsibility to the people he leads within the context of the organization.

For instance, some writers have suggested that a leader has no responsibility to the people because "the . . . leader is primarily a servant of God, not a servant of the sheep," and further, that any view contrary to this represents a "faulty" concept of leadership. It is my conviction that this view is one which is too often evident and practiced by Christian leaders. Scripture nowhere suggests that a leader's selection and subsequent accountability to the Heavenly Father legitimizes neglect of and inattention to the needs of the people being led. Our Lord, for example, while keenly aware of His Father's priorities, was careful not to ignore the oftentimes ignorant and simple concerns of His followers. He said part of His mission included being the servant of others. There are no caveats of exclusion for those who serve as leaders. Christ didn't give the Sermon on the Mount and then quickly add, "If you are a leader, you can ignore these teachings." Indeed, it would seem by implication that leaders have an even more significant responsibility for modeling these expectations. Voltaire, not a person to be accused of a Christian worldview, stated this responsibility in these words: "I am a leader, therefore I must follow."

Leaders have basically at least two choices regarding leadership style. They can choose, first, to pursue aggressive leadership—that is, where they are seen "as the people in charge, the bosses"—lead by fear and intimidation, and give only marginal attention to the genuine needs of the people.[3] This view asserts that only as long as it's good for the organization, only as long as it makes money or brings me customers, only as long as I am able to produce a better product, I'll attend to the more humane side of leadership.

The alternative view of leadership is one that states that before I assert the responsibilities assigned to my leadership position, I must first of all be a follower—a follower of Christ and, secondly, a follower of the people I lead—with careful attention to not only their needs but also to the contributions they can make which are vital if organizational goals are to be achieved and accomplished. This view of leadership is chosen not because it brings in new customers, more students, enhances church growth, or produces higher morale. Rather, this alternative is chosen because of the leader's desire to be obedient to the call of Christ in an organizational context.

It is not that the second alternative is chosen in ignorance of the "benefits" of the first alternative. Rather, the second alternative is chosen because of the belief that it best reflects the commands of Jesus. The first choice says something to the effect, "Well, if I have to work with people to achieve my ends, I'll do it." People within the organization, then, exist for the purpose of manipulation in the ways that provide the greatest benefit for the leader and presumably for the organization's mission. The second choice asserts, "This is my brother and sister in the Lord and I need to be committed to their welfare so that both their potential *and* that of the organization are achieved." These ideas and concepts are more fully developed in Part Two.

The third part of the book will focus on the more personal dimensions of leadership. Items to be included will involve the leader's spiritual walk, financial considerations (how much should I get paid?), family priorities, and other matters, including the troublesome issue of sexuality.

Michael Maccoby, in his book, *The Leader*, observes that "the old models of leadership no longer work. A new model of leadership is needed...." He observes that the "American public is dissatisfied with its leaders and confused about the kind of leader we need."[4] Tragedies resulting from strong leaders such as Jim Jones have done little to eliminate this confusion. It is my opinion, then, that Maccoby is right. New models of leadership are needed and what better place to look for them than in the pages of Scripture.

It is my hope that this book will be part of the process of helping to eliminate some of the confusion about leadership and to help return to a more biblically based model of the leader—not one where "top leadership is a fantasy of capricious power: the top man presses a button and something remarkable happens; he gives an order ... and it is obeyed"[5]—but, rather, where the leader is primarily a servant of Jesus who refuses to believe the idolatrous philosophy that the goals and needs of the organization require setting aside the biblical mandates for discipleship. This kind of leader begins the inquiry not with, "Can you run an organization like that?" but rather with, "What is God like and what does He desire of me and the people which He has entrusted to me?"[6]

PART ONE

LEADERSHIP AND LEADERSHIP CONCEPTS DEFINED AND DISCUSSED

"In the description of organizations, no word is more often used than leadership, and perhaps no word is used with such varied meanings."

DANIEL KATZ & ROBERT KAHN

One purpose of this book is to discuss the various concepts and ideas pertaining to leadership. In this part, concepts like leader, power, authority, and trust are presented and analyzed. While universal agreement is lacking as to what makes a good leader, there nevertheless must be some kind of consensus about what these concepts mean.

This part of the book may be viewed by some as more academic than the rest, particularly because of the variety of literature reviewed and discussed. Such discussion, however, is essential to understanding leadership and its many dimensions.

CHAPTER ONE

PRELIMINARY CONSIDERATIONS OF LEADERSHIP

Before the various other relationships involving the leader and the organization can be explored, the concept of leadership needs to be probed further. Just what is leadership? How does it differ from managership, and what might be its relationship to power and authority? These and other dimensions of leadership will be explored in this chapter. To flesh out our definition, a variety of literature will be explored.

According to Arthur Schlesinger, Jr., leadership is "the capacity to move, inspire, and mobilize masses of people."[1] Former U.S. Supreme Court Justice Arthur Goldberg defines leadership as "great ability and great opportunity greatly employed—an art, not a science and . . . largely intuitive."[2] Another author gives a rather simple definition: "one who guides or directs the activities of others." According to Ikenberry, "The most fundamental dimension of leadership is to nurture a set of values and beliefs that will answer the question *why?* Why do we do what we do? Why do we seek support? Why do we choose a particular course of action and resist another?"[3]

Some see leadership as pyramidal or hierarchical: "In this classic view, a chain of command lies at the heart of the operation. Information flows up the chain, orders come down. Obedience becomes the primary obligation of the employee and the giving of orders the responsibility of the leader."[4] This view is reflected in the observations of a Harvard Business School student as he described his perceptions of the kind of business leader most admired by his colleague students: "the tough, hands-on manager, someone who justifies his or her high pay by being the crisis-solver, the problem-fixer, the head-basher."[5]

However rigorous might be the attempt to define leadership, one must realize that the concept of leadership is not an exact science; if anything, it's like an inexact art. Gardner, for example, observes that:

> Any attempt to describe a process as complex as leadership inevitably makes it seem more orderly than it is. Leadership is not tidy. Decisions are made and then reversed. Misunderstandings are frequent, inconsistency inevitable. . . . Most of the time things are out of hand. No leader enjoys that reality, but every leader knows it.[6]

In addition, the observation should be made that there is no such thing as a model leader. Leaders come in a distinctive variety of shapes, sexes, colors, and ideas. The person successful in one organization or type of organization might be a dismal failure in another. Again, as Gardner has observed:

> I have in mind a superior leader in outdoor activities and sports who was quite incapable of leading in a bureaucratic setting. I have in mind a businessman with highly innovative ideas who has built a great corporation around those ideas but lacks any capacity to lead in unstructured situations.
>
> It may take one kind of leader to start a new enterprise and quite another to keep it going. Religious bodies, political parties, government agencies, the academic world—all offer distinctive contexts for leadership.[7]

In the context of Christian organizations, these differences will be readily recognized regarding the pastoral role, size of church, kind of denomination, and the like. This fact of "no one model" or type is a freeing thing for the Christian, as God reserves the option as to whom He will use in a variety of circumstances. Further, one cannot be excused from the biblical demands of leadership because "the right skills are not possessed." Moses, for example, thought that one of the essential skills for leadership was oratory.

Indeed, he used its lack in his own life as an excuse not to lead. After some additional and frustrating dialogue with God, a way was found for this problem to be addressed. The point to be made is that the record of Scripture is filled with stories of unlikely leaders, people whom we would quickly identify as leaders, but who, at the moment God called them for leadership duty, were convinced that they not only lacked the qualities for leadership but also felt they would be miserable leaders.

Notwithstanding this inability to pin down a precise definition of leadership, this chapter will focus on the objective of ascertaining some of its more tangible qualities. First, we will look at some of the writings of John Gardner. Few people have addressed the topic of leadership in greater depth than he. While his writings would not reflect a classic "textbook" approach to the topic, they do reflect a broad-based, experience-oriented collection of insights which the serious leader must consider. A second source will be the classic work, *The Social Psychology of Organizations* by Daniel Katz and Robert Kahn. Katz and Kahn discuss, on the one hand, characteristics of leadership, but their approach is always in the context of an organization. They would argue, for example, that anyone who is not a student of both leadership and at the same time a student of the organization is at best looking at only one side of the leadership coin. Other sources, in addition to these two, will be cited as appropriate.

Other threads which the reader will see repeatedly running throughout the leadership fabric, in addition to the concept of leadership, are those of power and authority. Indeed, it would be difficult to discuss leadership without also addressing these two concepts. As Ikenberry observes, "Leadership in its most fundamental form is the constructive exercise of power."[8] Thus, as this chapter develops, these two concepts will also be explored.

Gardner defines leadership as "the process of persuasion and example by which an individual (or leadership team) induces a group to take action that is in accord with the leader's purposes or the shared purposes of all."[9] The story of Moses leading the people from Egypt, for example, would fit this definition. The people to be led certainly desired to be out from under their Egyptian bondage. They had no plan, however, to effect this purpose until Moses, God's handpicked leader, came on the scene. Nehemiah also fits this description of leadership. In chapter two of the book which bears his name, he returned to Jerusalem to effect the completion of a God-given task. It can be implied from this story that God's people desired to see the walls rebuilt, but the task remained undone until this leader came on the scene. It's important to note from the accounts of Moses and Nehemiah that neither imposed himself on the people by a simple fiat such as, "God has appointed me to be your leader; now you be my followers." Rather, each provided evidence for the group about how he was called by God and equipped for the task. Moses could share his desert experience, including his confrontation with the living God at the burning bush. Nehemiah could share how King Artaxerxes had endorsed his mission in response to God's answered prayer. In brief, we see these two leaders as fitting Gardner's definition of leadership as spelled out earlier.

Gardner further notes that "holding a position of status does not make one a leader."[10] "There are government department heads, bishops, and corporate chief executive officers who could not lead a troop of Cub Scouts out of their pup tents."[11] And another writer had observed, "To be a leader one must have followers."[12] In this context, however, it should be noted that status is not irrelevant to leadership. As Gardner notes, "People expect . . . presidents . . . to lead, which heightens the possibility that they will."[13]

Another leadership distinctive which Gardner addresses is a substantive difference between "managers" and leaders. Some argue that one fundamental difference is that managers focus on making sure that things "get done right" while leaders focus on making sure that the "right things get done." Gardner is not so sure that indeed a major difference exists between managers and leaders. As he observes:

> Many writers on leadership are at considerable pains to distinguish between leaders and managers. In the process leaders generally end up looking like a cross between Napoleon and the Pied Piper, and managers like unimaginative clods. This troubles me. . . . Every time I encounter an utterly first-class manager he turns out to have quite a lot of the leader in him.[14]

Gardner, however, then proceeds to identify six ways in which leaders and leader/managers distinguish themselves from the general run of managers:

> 1. They think longer term . . . ; 2. They look beyond the unit they are heading and grasp its relationship to larger realities . . . ; 3. They reach and influence constituents beyond their jurisdictions and boundaries . . . ; 4. They put heavy emphasis on the intangibles of vision, values and motivation, and understand intuitively the non-rational and unconscious elements in the leader-constituent (follower) interaction; 5. They have the political skill to cope with the conflicting requirements of multiple constituencies; and 6. They think in terms of renewal.[15]

GARDNER'S LEADERSHIP TASKS

Gardner argues for at least nine critical tasks of a leader. *First*, the leader has the responsibility to "envision goals."[16] By this he means the ability to set goals and to create a vision of what the people or the organization can achieve. Time and time again we see the leaders in the Old Testament envisioning goals for their people. When people saw the walls around Jericho and complained, "No, we can't," Joshua said, "Yes, we can." When the Israelites were faced with Goliath and said, "No, we can't," David responded with a vigorous, "Yes, we can." When ten of the spies told the Israelites they could not capture Canaan because of the giants and other obstacles, Moses, Joshua, and Caleb said, "Yes, we can."

The *second* task Gardner identifies is the need for the leader to "affirm values."[17] As he observes:

> A great civilization is a drama lived in the minds of a people. It is a shared vision; it is shared norms, expectations and purposes. When one thinks of the world's great civilizations, the most vivid images that crowd in on us are of the monuments left behind. . . . But in truth all the physical splendor was the merest by-product. The civilizations themselves, from the beginning to end, existed in the minds of men and women.[18]

The values shared by the people Moses led came from a

variety of sources, the most important of which were the Ten Commandments. Over and over Moses had to remind the people not only of shared values but the sole foundation for those shared values—trust in the Almighty God.

Gardner's *third* leadership task is that of "motivating."[19] Observes Gardner: "Leaders do not normally create motivation out of thin air. They unlock or channel existing motives."[20] It is for these reasons, for example, that a leader must attend to the goals, dreams, and needs of the people being led. Motivation cannot be superimposed on the group. "Any group," says Gardner, "has a great tangle of motives. Effective leaders tap those motives that serve the purposes of collective action in pursuit of significant shared goals."[21] One of the methods constantly used by Moses in this regard was to continually identify for the people the blessings which would result if obedience to God were forthcoming. Just as important, however, were the negative consequences that would follow if obedience were not the chosen course. And negative motivations can produce positive actions as well as positive motivations can produce positive actions.

Gardner further observes that "positive views of the future must be tempered by a measure of tough-minded realism."[22] Neither Moses nor Joshua suggested, for example, that the Promised Land could be taken without some degree of difficulty, e.g., fighting. What they did assure the people, however, was that God was on their side and that they would prevail.

A *fourth* leadership task identified by Gardner is "managing."[23] While he doesn't necessarily see this as the primary role of leadership, Gardner does see it as an indispensable part of the task of leadership. Management items that he identifies, for example, include those of planning, priority-setting, agenda-setting, decision-making, and exercising political judgment.

In the Old Testament, for example, careful attention was given to not only the concept of worship but also *how* people were to worship. The various sacrifices, offerings, and procedures the people were to follow in a host of areas were painstakingly and meticulously spelled out. Many times, after consulting the Lord, Moses told the people how to get water and where to get bread. These activities are representative of basic management tasks.

A *fifth* task of leadership is to achieve "workable unity."[24]

Gardner does not suggest that this task will be achieved when total organizational uniformity is present or when there is a total absence of conflict. In fact, he believes that some conflict will be inevitable: "Indeed one could argue that willingness to engage in battle when necessary is a *sine qua non* of leadership." Gardner holds that this task includes the concern for and ability to resolve conflicts and the need to build trust in the organization.

The subject of unity in Scripture is a rich one. Many of the Apostle Paul's letters discussed this very important topic. And Christ Himself, as expressed in His prayer to His Father just prior to His death, made the subject of unity a significant part of the prayer:

> My prayer is not for them alone. I pray also for those who will believe in me through their message, that all of them may be one, Father, just as you are in me and I am in you. May they also be in us so that the world may believe that you have sent me. I have given them the glory that you gave me, that they may be one as we are one: I in them and you in me. May they be brought to complete unity to let the world know that you sent me and have loved them even as you have loved me (John 17:20-23).

Indeed, He stated that the evidence to the world that He was sent by the Father would be to have the world see believers brought to complete unity.

A *sixth* task of leadership is that of "explaining."[25] By explaining Gardner suggests here the need for sharing information about what is going on and why. Gardner sees a strong similarity between the explaining function of leaders and the teaching function of leaders: "Teaching and leading are distinguishable occupations, but every great leader is clearly teaching—and every great teacher is leading."[26] One of the primary roles of Moses as a leader was Moses as a teacher. Time and time again he called the people together to teach them the ways of the Lord. And he called on the people to also be teachers—of their own children. Children likewise were to be attentive to their parents' instruction: "Listen, my son, to your father's instruction and do not forsake your mother's teaching" (Proverbs 1:8).

A *seventh* task of leadership is to "serve as a symbol."[27] Any leader—whether a pastor, CEO, foreman, or teacher, to name a few—has faced the issue of being identified primarily as a symbol. My grade-school teacher was a symbol to me of every good thing there was to know about teaching and learning. When I saw her in the store she was still my teacher and I expected her to act in a certain way. The same could be said about a host of other leadership positions. The leader who refuses to recognize this symbolic role, who insists always on being his own person, will indeed face a rocky road. Observes Gardner: "Leaders can rarely afford the luxury of speaking for themselves alone."[28] Moses was very much aware of his symbolic role in this regard. So too were the high priests. When Moses went to the top of Mount Sinai, for example, he went there not just for himself but on behalf of his people. The commandments he received were not just for his benefit, but for all the people's benefit.

The *eighth* task of leadership that Gardner identifies is that of "representing the group."[29] This representational function or task is probably most easily identified in the political realm when a leader from one country sits down with the leader of another country to negotiate some treaty or agreement. A ready illustration of this role in the Scripture is when Joshua negotiated a treaty with the Gibeonites. God had instructed Joshua to wipe out the neighboring countries, yet the Gibeonites perpetrated a successful ruse which fooled Joshua. As the people's representative, however, he was bound, once the ruse was discovered, to abide by its terms. In the case of Moses, this representational role was clearly identified by his father-in-law during a visit: "Listen now to me and I will give you some advice, and may God be with you. You must be the people's representative before God and bring their disputes to him" (Exodus 18:19).

The *ninth* task of leadership identified by Gardner is the task of "renewing."[30] What Gardner has in mind is that organizations are always changing. As a result, previously valid methods may, at some time in the future, be discarded. He argues that because of change, the organization must always be seeking to be self-renewed so that its purposes and goals, even though achieved by different methods, will nevertheless remain intact. According to Gardner:

Little by little, preoccupation with method, technique and

procedure gains a subtle dominance *over* the whole process of goal seeking. How it is done becomes more important than whether it is done. Means triumph over ends. Form triumphs over spirit. Method is enthroned. Men become prisoners of their procedures, and organizations that were designed to achieve some goal become obstacles in the path to that goal.[31]

An extremely vivid illustration of this task relates to the New Testament shift to include the Gentiles in the church when previously only Jewish believers were included. Paul was more sensitive to the renewing function in this specific context than was Peter, but with the help of a heavenly vision, Peter too caught the message even though he continued to struggle with all of the ramifications of it.

Before turning to the works of Katz and Kahn, I want to note one other concept that Gardner identifies—the concept of the leadership team. He argues that a person will be a better leader if he or she is part of a leadership team:

> Most of the leadership that can be called effective involves a number of individuals acting in a team relationship. . . . Most ventures fare better if one person is in charge—but not as a solo performer, not as a giant surrounded by pygmies.[32]

Gardner argues for the leadership team concept for several reasons. First, just as the organization is constantly changing, so too is the leader. And the leader who is surrounded with a team of key players, each of whom possesses different yet complementary strengths is well positioned to keep up with and ahead of the needs of the organization. Second, the leadership structure is constantly in a state of adjustment. While every organization has an official organizational chart, most members of an organization know the informal as well as the formal levels of access. As Gardner observes, "Everyone understands the 'kitchen cabinet' phenomenon."[33] Again, leadership that is dispersed is well positioned to deal with both this formal and informal structure. Third, just as people within the organization are changing, so too is the organization's external environment. And leadership that is dispersed can be in tune with these changes.

KATZ AND KAHN ON LEADERSHIP

One of the foremost sources on the nature of the organization in the context of leadership is the classic, *The Social Psychology of Organizations* by Daniel Katz and Robert Kahn. This book ought to be required reading for any person who aspires to and/or who serves in a position of leadership. One basic assumption in much of their work is that the study of leadership is incomplete without an understanding of how organizations function as organizations. The leader who understands how organizations function, and more specifically, how his or her organization functions, optimizes the probabilities for effective leadership.

As Katz and Kahn discuss leadership, they identify the three ways the concept has typically been presented: "as the attribute of a position, as the characteristic of a person, and as a category of behavior. To be a superior is to occupy a position of leadership, and to be a company president is to occupy a position of greater leadership."[34] They also suggest that leadership is a relational concept—"the influencing agent and the persons influenced. Without followers there can be no leader."[35] Further, they suggest that leadership is more than role performance. They see the organizational leader as one who is willing to (and usually does) go far beyond the usual expectations of role performance: "We consider the essence of organizational leadership to be the influential increment over and above mechanical compliance with the routine directives of the organization."[36]

These authors identify several reasons why leadership is needed. First, any kind of organization has an incomplete structure. People usually know the difference between how the organization is supposed to work and how in fact it does work. Unless one is committed to a multi-volume description of organizational intricacies (and some Christian organizations are), there are usually some gaps between practice and structure that require ongoing interpretation, adaptation, embellishment, or omission. The effective leader helps in this process.

One of the primary concerns of Jesus as presented in the Gospels was that the Jewish leaders had gone overboard in this area. Their efforts to be precise and tight with their religious regulations—to make everything nice and neat—took the heart and reason out of the reason for the regulation in the first place. As Katz and Kahn observe: "The concrete case always needs something of interpretation and adaptation, embellishment or thoughtful omission."[37] Jesus did this as a leader and it got Him into trouble. As a leader, however, He thought it well worth the trouble.

A second reason for leadership in an organization, according to Katz and Kahn, is that the external conditions under which the organization must function are always changing.[38] The leader then serves as a viable link to the outside boundary areas or conditions. Organizations, including churches, are vitally impacted in their programs by things that happen beyond their walls or even communities. Mission programs and the need to feed the hungry are but two examples. Concern about legislation, whether on the topic of pornography or abortion, is another. One of the Apostle Paul's functions and priorities was to keep geographically distant groups of Christians aware of each other's needs. He was pleased to no end when he saw a generous response on the part of one group to the needs of another. In this role Paul served as a leader.

A third reason for leadership is that organizations themselves are always changing.[39] New goals are identified and priorities established. And adjustments to organizational structure follow. One of the needs for leadership is to coordinate and direct this change. When the early New Testament church was getting started, it had to make a distinction between elders and deacons because of rapidly changing needs and new priorities. Moses had to reorganize his management style because of the changing needs of the people he led.

According to Katz and Kahn, the initiation of change within an organization "is the most challenging of all organizational tasks and rarely occurs without strong pressure outside the organization."[40] Pressure from outside the organization can come in a variety of ways—a vibrant church opens across the street; the old stodgy church gets a dynamic new pastor; or a financial crisis occurs. Examples are numerous, but I want to comment briefly on this last one. A leader usually laments hardship when it impacts the organization. In my work as college president, this might mean lower enrollments or a bad year financially. These circumstances, however discouraging and troublesome, provide prime opportunities for making organizational changes probably not possible absent the crisis. Leaders should be very sensitive to not only the need to correct the circumstance that created the crisis (assuming it was not the leader who created it in the first place), but should also be alert to the kind of changes which might enhance the organization and which could not otherwise be made in the absence of an externally generated problem. Again, though, the point must be made—without strong outside pressure, change within the organization will be extremely difficult.

According to Katz and Kahn, those leaders who have been effective at organizational change have possessed two qualities, one cognitive—systemic perspective, and the other affective—charisma.[41]

Systemic perspective means the ability to see the way each part of the organization relates to the others and how the organization itself relates to the larger world beyond. In a church setting, for example, it means the pastoral staff is alert to how the teenagers relate to the older folks, how the families with young children relate to grandparents, how the elder board relates to the deacon board, and how the music program relates to the Sunday School program. They must also be aware of how their local church relates to other churches within the denomination and/or to other churches within the community or region. In the university setting, the president must be alert to how the various constituent parts relate together: the faculty to the board; the administration to the students; the administration to the board; the alumni to the administration; the school to the community; the school to other schools within the given state or region. In brief, systemic perspective is important for leaders, and critically important if change is desired.

With regard to charisma, as Katz and Kahn note: "The top organizational leader, who possesses legitimate power and controls rewards and sanctions, can mobilize more support for policies if he or she can generate charisma, that magical aura with which people sometimes endow their leaders."[42] According to Katz and Kahn, "Charisma is not the objective assessment by followers of the leader's ability to meet their specific needs. It is a means by which people abdicate responsibility for any consistent, tough-minded evaluation of the outcome of specific policies. They put their trust in their leader who will somehow take care of things."[43] David Whetten argues that "charismatic leaders use their powers of persuasion to convince others to follow a course of action articulated by the leader."[44] Many times people assume that a leader is charismatic, meaning that he or she is "blessed" with a given personality type. Non-charismatic leaders look almost with envy at this type of personality and secretly wish that it was theirs as well. Few people, however, view charisma as something that the people themselves give to the leader and further, that charismatic leadership is characterized by abdication of responsibility on the part of the people and psychological distance between leaders and followers. It shouldn't come as a surprise that many leaders who are described as charismatic maintain distance between themselves and their followers. They do so because, "Day-to-day intimacy destroys illusion."[45] Jim Jones and Adolf Hitler were certainly charismatic leaders, and yet few in leadership positions see them as persons to be emulated.

A fourth reason for leadership is that the primary makeup of the organization is people. Organizations consist of "human origin and human embodiment."[46] As Katz and Kahn observe: "Only people can be members of an organization, but people are not only members of organizations, and above all not members of only one organization. Human membership in an organization is segmental in nature; it involves only a part of the person. Other activities and affiliations fill other hours, make demands on energies, gratify needs. These extra-organizational and other-organizational aspects of a person's life affect behavior of the person in the organization, and changes in these aspects of life produce changes in his or her behavior on the job."[47]

Effective leaders are alert to the competing demands on the performance requirements within the organization. Leaders are alert to the fact that "people mature, age, and otherwise assimilate the continuing experience of living."[48] Further, people eventually wear out. "Each such change has organizational ramifications and represents a kind of . . . demand that cannot be wholly predicted. . . . "[49] Again, the leader must be sensitive to these kinds of changes, including those he or she may undergo in the same way.

Scripture well illustrates the point that people change and leaders change. The Israelites were a different people under the leadership of Moses and Joshua than they were under subsequent leaders. The apostles performed differently after Jesus rose from the dead and returned to heaven than they did while He was still on earth. In the context of our families, our priorities as parents are different when the children are all under age ten than when all of them are in their teens. People change, leaders change, and organizations change. Leaders must be sensitive to these kinds of changes and respond accordingly.

Katz and Kahn share Gardner's ambivalence about whether or not there is a crystal clear distinction between the leader and the manager/administrator. As they note: "Organizations do not achieve greatness on the basis of their adequacy in handling daily administrative chores, but unless these are taken care of, the organization deteriorates."[50] They also observe the neglect in given organizations "in which the top leaders spend almost all their time discussing policies and plans and are out of touch with the daily requirements of organizational life."[51]

They argue further that one key difference between those organizations that are successful from those that are not is that the leadership function is dispersed throughout the organization. As they note: "People have greater feelings of commitment to decisions in which they have a part . . . ; and the wide distribution of the leadership function is likely to improve the quality of decisions. . . . "[52] As they observe, "Few indeed are the organizational disasters that occurred unforeseen—by someone."[53] Recall, for a moment, Gardner's call for dispersed leadership and connect it now with this observation. What is being stated by implication is that an organization that has no dispersed leadership, or alternatively, where an organization does this poorly, the organization itself may be in serious danger. Why? It may be unaware of impending problems or disasters that everyone else knows about; poor decision-making may dominate; and continuity in leadership is imperiled. In other words, an organization may be so tightly built around its leadership that when that leadership is no longer "on board," the organization will not stay intact. Dispersed leadership avoids this peril.

It is my observation that many Christian organizations do not do a good job in the area of dispersed leadership. One strong leader (this is particularly the case in family-run organizations) or several strong senior-level administrators literally run the whole show. Very little input is sought or welcomed from other levels of employees. The question, therefore, can legitimately be asked: what will happen when those family leaders or those senior-level administrators are off the scene?

And just why do family-led organizations dislike dispersed

leadership? Reasons vary, but a primary one is based on the assumption that God has entrusted the family and its head, and them alone, to be the keepers of the vision. And since they have been entrusted with the vision, and since other persons might adulterate the vision, leadership in this kind of organization is tightly held by a small, select number of people. From a very pragmatic perspective, these organizations are all doomed to go out of existence on the death of the founder or shortly thereafter. After all, no one else has been entrusted the vision by God. Not surprisingly—since God may choose, after the death of the founder, to entrust the vision to another family member (perhaps the wife or a son)—one must also question the theological assumptions on which the organization is built. Does God entrust only a few special people with the real work of God? Does He keep all the rest of us in a constant state of visionary ignorance? How does the concept of spiritual unity fit here? What about the concept of the body of Christ? While it is true that throughout the Old Testament God gave special leaders a vision or divine mission (e.g., Moses, Abraham, Daniel), such was done usually in the context of a sparsity of others who were willing to take God at His promises.

Moses was preoccupied with running the whole show until his father-in-law Jethro paid him a visit. Jethro observed the situation, assessed it properly, and said Moses' workload was too heavy:

> What you are doing is not good. You and these people who come to you will only wear yourselves out. The work is too heavy for you; you cannot handle it alone (Exodus 18:17-18).

Thereafter, he suggested a new dispersed leadership structure in which Moses became an even more effective leader:

> "But select capable men from all the people—men who fear God, trustworthy men who hate dishonest gain—and appoint them as officials over thousands, hundreds, fifties and tens. Have them serve as judges for the people at all times, but have them bring every difficult case to you; the simple cases they can decide themselves. That will make your load lighter, because they will share it with you. If you do this

and God so commands, you will be able to stand the strain, and all these people will go home satisfied." Moses listened to his father-in-law and did everything he said (Exodus 18:21-24).

Alternatively, Joshua apparently did not effectively use a dispersed leadership style because after he was off the scene, the very things he stood for vanished, and a generation grew up who knew not God. Who says it can't happen again? Leaders who are committed to a long-term view of the organization will be practitioners of dispersed leadership.

CHAPTER
TWO

POWER, AUTHORITY, AND TRUST

One cannot very well discuss the issue of leadership without also discussing the concepts of power, authority, and trust. In this chapter we will discuss these three concepts, and in the process review some of the related literature.

LEADERSHIP AND POWER

Kast and Rosenzweig give us one of the better definitions of power:

> Power is the capability of doing or affecting something. It implies the ability to influence others. In its most general sense, power denotes (1) the ability . . . to produce a certain occurrence or (2) the influence exerted by a man or group, through whatever means, over the conduct of others in intended ways. . . .[1]

According to them, "While power underlies the entire spectrum of ways to influence behavior, its everyday connotation leans toward the persuasive-coercive end of the spectrum. Although power is the general ability to produce a certain occurrence, it implies the force, if necessary, to control or command others."[2] They note that "if coercion or the application of force is ineffective, there is no power."[3]

According to Kast and Rosenzweig, there are three kinds of

power: physical power, material power, and symbolic power.[4] Physical power is most readily thought of in the context of the police or a military organization. These types of entities have the power to harm, incarcerate, or even to take one's life in certain circumstances. An example of material power could be the leading financier of an organization. All CEOs know the power of a donor who insists on using his or her donation to manipulate the organization toward a particular direction or to pursue a particular purpose. An example of symbolic power would be motivating people to do their best in order to help the organization achieve its goals.

In the same way that he has written about leadership, John Gardner has also provided some useful analyses on the subject of power. He notes as follows:

> Power is not to be confused with status or prestige. It is the capacity to ensure the outcomes one wishes and to prevent those one does not wish. . . . Power as we are now speaking of it—power in the social dimension—is simply the capacity to bring about certain intended consequences in the behavior of others.[5]

Gardner distinguishes between leaders and power holders: "Leaders always have a measure of power. But many power holders have no trace of leadership."[6]

As Kast and Rosenzweig imply, some see power in a negative and almost evil light. As Gardner observes:

> In this country—and in most other democracies—power has such a bad name that many good people persuade themselves that they want nothing to do with it. The ethical and spiritual apprehensions are understandable. But one cannot abjure power.[7]

He comments further:

> To say a leader is preoccupied with power is like saying a tennis player is preoccupied with making shots his opponent cannot return. Of course leaders are preoccupied with power! The significant questions are: What means do they

use to gain it? How do they exercise it? To what ends do they exercise it?[8]

Simple reflection about the life and ministry of Christ on earth suggests that He not only had power—indeed, He is the most powerful person ever to have walked the face of the earth—but He exercised power appropriately and toward appropriate ends. His life provides the positive example about how power can be used and ought to be used. If a leader wants to use his power for purposes of self-aggrandizement, what would Jesus have done? If a leader wants to use power to strike back at those who falsely and maliciously misrepresent him, what would Jesus have done? Jesus' words recorded in Mark 10:42-44 bear repeating:

> You know that those who are regarded as rulers of the Gentiles lord it over them, and their high officials exercise authority over them. Not so with you. Instead, whoever wants to become great among you must be your servant, and whoever wants to be first must be slave of all.

It's not enough, however, for leaders to eschew power. As Gardner notes, "Power lodges somewhere."[9] The key issues, then, for the Christian leader include submitting that power to the lordship of Christ, to use power the right way, and further, to use it for God-honoring ends.

I want to emphasize that the leader needs to avoid the trap of concluding that, since power is directed to an appropriate end, the processes of *how* power is exercised can be ignored. We must go past processes and look still further to motive. Time and time again, "religious" people in the Old Testament were castigated by God for impure motives:

> I hate, I despise your religious feasts; I cannot stand your assemblies. Even though you bring me burnt offerings and grain offerings, I will not accept them. Though you bring choice fellowship offerings, I will have no regard for them. Away with the noise of your songs! I will not listen to the music of your harps (Amos 5:21-23).

Other biblical references to the matter of motive include:

For the word of God is living and active. Sharper than any double-edged sword, it penetrates even to dividing soul and spirit, joints and marrow; it judges the thoughts and attitudes of the heart (Hebrews 4:12).

Then hear from heaven, your dwelling place. Forgive, and deal with each man according to all he does, since you [the Lord] know his heart (for you alone know the hearts of men) (2 Chronicles 6:30).

Therefore judge nothing before the appointed time; wait till the Lord comes. He will bring to light what is hidden in darkness and will expose the motives of men's hearts. At that time each will receive his praise from God (1 Corinthians 4:5).

Therefore, as I exercise power in leadership, I need to be alert to my innermost motives governing its exercise, the ways in which power is exercised, and the ends or purposes for which it is exercised.

It is vital, notes Gardner, to make sure that leaders hold to high standards of accountability. He notes Lord Acton's assertion: "Power tends to corrupt; absolute power corrupts absolutely."[10] He observes, and I want to underscore his emphasis, that because many in our society view power as the essence of wickedness, Lord Acton's remark is generally misquoted as "Power corrupts" rather than quoted in its correct form: "Power tends to corrupt." Simply put, leaders ought to welcome efforts by boards to insist on leadership accountability, for accountability is an important control for making sure power and authority are properly handled. Alternatively, too many "safeguards" can make a leader totally ineffective. As Gardner notes, "When accountable leaders are stripped of power, the people lose power."[11]

Richard Foster likewise stresses this important connection between accountability and power:

Those who are accountable to no one are especially susceptible to the corrupting influence of power. . . . Today, most media preachers and itinerant evangelists suffer . . . from the same lack of accountability that the wandering prophets of the sixth century did.[12]

Says Foster, "What we must see is the wrongness of those who think they are always right."[13]

In her very helpful book, *The Religion of Power*, Cheryl Forbes discusses the concept of power. To her way of thinking, power is defined as follows:

> Insistence on what we want for no other reason than that we want it; it means making other people follow us despite their own wishes. Power is assumed, insensitive, dehumanizing, and ultimately destructive.[14]

Forbes clearly has in mind here the kind of coercive corporate power described by Pascale and Athos:

> American assumptions about power are important in shaping managerial style. One such assumption is that an executive needs to get all the power he can, needs to use it openly, even blatantly, to keep it, and should not act in any way that reduces his capacity to impact others directly.[15]

Forbes sees *power* as something to be "delivered from" rather than to be sought after: "Christians must say no to power, individually and corporately. A decision for power is antithetical to a desire for God."[16] Conversely, she sees *authority* as "positive and usually involves a conferred right within strictly controlled bounds. It is a temporary recognition or a temporary state of 'inchargeness.' "[17]

For the Christian, Forbes' argument is clearly slanted in the right direction. I agree with her implicit assumption that too many Christians are power hungry and that, in their pursuit of power, they end up violating all kinds of biblical commands. It seems to me, however, that she has taken her position further than necessary. For example, while she seemingly applauds the concept of authority and eschews that of power, she fails to note that there can be no authority *without* power, since authority is legitimatized and/or institutionalized power. Furthermore, we need to remember that Christ is total power (He also had and therefore spoke with authority); that He properly serves as the model to leaders who need to exercise power; and that before His ascension He told us we would need to be comfortable with a particular type of spiritual power ("You will receive power," Acts 1:8). As Denny has observed:

> Nobody has ever possessed more power than Christ. And yet, he rejected it, preferring instead to be a powerless sheep among wolves. The disciples wanted to know which of them was the greatest, and He answered by washing their feet, a task normally reserved for the least.[18]

Further, Forbes' concept of power ("making people follow us despite their own wishes"[19]) would produce chaos in almost any organization. It would enthrone within the organization a kind of "everybody-can-do-whatever-they-wish-to-do" mentality. People who choose to be employed by an organization have a responsibility to make sure their own wishes coincide with the wishes or mission of the organization. Paul had every expectation that the New Testament churches would respond to the various expectations spelled out by the Holy Spirit's leading. Indeed, when people wanted to follow their own wishes rather than those Paul felt were imperatives of the Spirit and/or of the Lord Himself, he specifically demanded that the people line up with these principles against their own wishes. Further, he laid down specific disciplinary actions for those who insisted on pursuing their own wishes. While Forbes' definition of power—at least to my way of thinking—misses the mark, it would fit as an example of power gone awry.

LEADERSHIP AND AUTHORITY

It is difficult to discuss the issue of power without also discussing the issue of authority, even though they are different concepts. According to Charles Colson, "Power and authority must not be confused. Power is the ability to affect one's ends or purposes in the world. Authority is having not only the power (might), but the right to affect one's purpose. Power is often maintained by naked force; authority springs from a moral foundation. Mother Teresa is the best living example. She spends her life helping the powerless die with dignity; yet few people command more authority worldwide."[20] Colson cautions us that "worldly power—whether measured by buildings, budgets, baptisms or access to the White House—is more often the enemy than the ally of godliness."[21] The concept of authority, then, appears on the same continuum as power but at a different place. According to Kast and Rosenzweig, "Authority is institutionalized power . . . the institutionalized right to limit choice. . . . It is the institutionalized right to employ power."[22]

Just as there are different kinds of power, there are also different kinds of authority. Again, Kast and Rosenzweig identify two: traditional and rational-legal.[23] Traditional authority evolves as "informal status and role systems become stabilized over time. It is exemplified by the phrase, 'it has always been this way.' Over a period of time the system evolves to the point where directives are carried out by subordinates without question. . . . The traditions in the system may be handed down explicitly in written form or implicitly in a manner similar to folklore."[24] Traditions, according to these authors, play a significant and legitimate role in any organization.

Rational-legal authority is when the tradition and/or a variety of other organizational practices and procedures become codified. In society at large, this authority appears in the form of legislation. In organizations, it appears in the form of handbooks and manuals of procedures and/or operations.[25] Kast and Rosenzweig further observe that organizations may combine the various kinds of authority to achieve the desired effect:

> Most organizations have a mixture of . . . authority underlying the influence system used to secure coordinated effort. . . . Some may be influenced . . . by traditional relationships which have evolved over a period of time. . . . Rational/legal authority can be invoked to elicit desired behavior on the part of participants who are not inclined to contribute willingly.[26]

Observations similar to those reflected in the writings of Kast and Rosenzweig appear elsewhere. According to Gardner: "Authority is legitimized power, i.e., a mandate to exercise power in a certain sphere. It is official or traditional sanction for individuals occupying specified positions to perform certain directive acts. . . . The meter maid has authority but not necessarily leadership.[27] Psychiatrist John White sees a similar distinction: "If you have authority, you have the right to do something. . . . Power, on the other hand, gives you the ability to control."[28] In other words, if I have power, I have the ability to control; but, if I lack authority to do so, I cannot do so legitimately.

The relationship among power, authority, and leadership is important *and* quite complex. To paraphrase Gardner, neither authority nor power make one a leader. There are those who have both power and authority but who have no willing followers. Again, the comments of Pascale and Athos are helpful:

> The consistent picture of the effective leader is the one who adopts the style of a "superfollower," who serves with his followers' blessing and consent, and who is able to inspire because he is first able to respond to their needs and concerns. Power in this context means the ability to get things done, to mobilize resources, and to draw on what is necessary to accomplish goals. Power is thus more akin to "mastery" than to "domination" or "control."[29]

The issue for the Christian leader, then, is neither an undue concern for power for its own sake nor authority for its own sake. Rather, the issue is, "How can I exercise God-given power and authority in a way to help the organization which He has entrusted to me achieve His purposes and goals?" Again, how I use power and authority as a leader becomes just as important as the ends sought through the use of both power and authority.

LEADERSHIP AND TRUST

When one becomes a leader in an organization—any organization, whether a church, a college, a business—there are a variety of voices saying, "Trust me." In a college situation, for example, the faculty want the trust of the administration and vice versa. The alumni want to be trusted by the administration and vice versa, and so on down the line. Everybody wants to be trusted.

The theology of biblical Christianity is heavily impacted with the need to "trust in Christ as Saviour." We are frequently instructed to make sure we trust the Lord:

> Trust in the Lord with all your heart and lean not on your own understanding; in all your ways acknowledge him, and he will make your paths straight (Proverbs 3:5-6).

> Trust in the Lord and do good; dwell in the land and enjoy safe pasture. Delight yourself in the Lord and he will give you the desires of your heart. Commit your way to the Lord; trust in him and he will do this (Psalm 37:3-5).

While the intent here is not to flesh out the meaning of trust in the theological sense, it is the intent to discuss such in an organizational context. Before further considering the matter of trust, some basic definitions are called for.

According to Webster, trust involves the following ideas:

> assured reliance on the character, ability, strength, or truth of someone or something; one in which confidence is placed; something committed or entrusted to one to be used or cared for in the interest of another.[30]

When I trust someone, what I am in essence saying is that, in matters affecting my welfare, I know the one trusted will be concerned about and will diligently work for the betterment of my interests. Furthermore, I need not use extraordinary measures in order for that commitment to be carried out. This is the idea expressed by John Gardner: "A loyal constituency is won when people, consciously, judge the leader to be capable of solving their problems and meeting their needs. . . . "[31]

Managing this seeming paradox of trust is critically important for the leader. All constituencies must have a mutual respect and trust for each other. Having power and authority is not enough. As Gardner notes:

> There is much to be gained for any leader in winning the trust of constituents. . . . Leaders must not only forge bonds of trust between themselves and their constituents, they must create a climate of trust throughout the system over which they preside. Trust is not the only glue that holds a human group together, but when it dissolves, the capacity of the group to function effectively is seriously impaired.[32]

According to Louis Barnes of Harvard University, trust in an organization is more important to its functioning than is either authority or power. Further, trust is easily destroyed, but perhaps, just as importantly, trust can be easily created and/or restored. Barnes notes that leaders and their followers "behave according to their assumptions of how the world works—whether, for instance, it is a kind or cruel place."[33]

I remember well the story I heard in college which illustrates this point. Mr. Smith had a house go up for sale on either side of his house. When the house on the left was sold, its new, out-of-town owner came to visit Smith and while there raised this simple query: "What kind of people live in this town?" Smith quickly responded, "Well, what kind of people live in the town where you came from?" After some thought, the new neighbor said that the people in his old town were picky, unfriendly, and not very helpful. Said Smith, "Those are the kind of people you're gonna find here." The other new neighbor also visited Smith and raised the same question as his predecessor. Smith responded in kind. The neighbor's response pleased Smith: "Where I come from people are loving, kind, extremely friendly, and most helpful." Said Smith, "Those are the kind of people you're gonna find here." Each of the views of the neighbors in this story, while perhaps humorous, indicate, assuming each is a manager or leader, the degree to which trust will be built in the organizations he leads.

According to Barnes, trust is readily destroyed when leaders hold to three seemingly harmless assumptions:

> First, that important issues naturally fall into two opposing camps, exemplified by either/or thinking; second, that hard data and facts are better than what appear to be soft ideas and speculation, exemplified in the "hard drives out soft" rule; and finally, that the world in general is an unsafe place, exemplified by a person's having a pervasive mistrust of the universe around him or her.[34]

It is Barnes' observation that while these assumptions seem simple enough, when leaders combine all three, the long term organizational impact can be "very destructive" to the issue of trust. His observations bear scrutiny and are worthy of further discussion.

1. *Either/or thinking.* According to Barnes, this assumption reflects the tendency to believe only two primary options exist in any decision milieu. Practical observation suggests that a given problem may have multifold solutions. The leader who is an

either/or practitioner, along with the related organization who practices it, tends to limit the range of options for resolving difficulty. Furthermore,the options presented, usually two, soon become symbols which represent polarized entities. Thereafter, the polarization evolves into sides such as unions versus management, black versus white, theory versus practice, us versus them. In a church situation, the sides can take many shapes—the young versus the old, the big givers versus the small givers, and oldtimers versus the newcomers. Barnes suggests by implication, therefore, that leaders need to avoid either/or thinking, not only to minimize the unnecessary polarization which results from symbolic concerns but, more importantly, so that the organization is open to other options.

2. *Hard is better than soft.* As an extension of either/or thinking, Barnes argues that this second false assumption is built around a premise something like the following: "If I have data for supporting my recommendation and you base your recommendation only on feelings or intuition, then my recommendation is superior to or better than your decision and my recommendation should prevail." Since I want my recommendations to prevail, I search for hard data or facts or numbers rather than searching my feelings or intuition or other more abstract possibilities.

According to Pascale and Athos, the Western management mindset is dominated by "hard" managers:

> American managers tend to overfocus on the "hard" elements. . . . Some of the best work done in business schools in recent decades has been in advancing our understanding of the "cold triangle" of strategy, structure, and systems. Each one and the relationships among the three are particularly susceptible to analytical, quantitative, logical, and systematic investigation. In short, "science" of one kind or another, rigorous observation and conceptualization—thinking, if you prefer—were required. That's what business schools value. That's how professors get rewarded. And that's what fits our culture's central beliefs about managing.[35]

What these authors observe is that Western culture is dominated by this "hard" mindset while other cultures are more open to a "soft" mindset. "Hard versus soft," then, is more a phenomenon of culture than it is a requirement for good management. Pascale and Athos, moreover, caution against ignoring the "soft" parts of organizational management:

> In short, the . . . soft elements can no longer be regarded as frosting on the corporate cake. They are indispensable parts of any corporate commitment to long-term success.[36]

In brief, in an era of high tech, when data are quickly generated, it's quite easy to become enamored with the idea that hard is really better than soft.

This faulty assumption poses other dangers that the leader needs to be concerned about. First, little "hard" thinking is done about the future. Since the future is not as easily quantifiable as the present, few attempts are made to face it. As a result, random, short-term decisions, presumably based on "harder" data, predominate over long-term considerations. A second concern is that "hard-nosed" decisions tend to acquire their own momentum and are difficult for a leader to reverse even when "everyone" knows or feels that the decision is wrong.

Interestingly, trust appears to be a soft variable.

3. *Nice guys finish last.* This assumption "holds that the world is a dangerous place requiring that a person adopt a position of pervasive mistrust to survive."[37] In an organizational context, this view assumes Darwinian or "survival of the fittest" overtones: "I need to get the other guy before he gets me. Our organization needs to come up with the creative plan or program first; otherwise, our competitor, whether the college or the church next door, will take away all our potential students or potential parishioners." Such an assumption negatively impacts the trust level within an organization.

ENHANCING TRUST

Barnes' research efforts suggest that one key variable in the ability of an organization to solve problems is a high level of trust. If this is the case, what can a leader to do enhance trust? According to Barnes, leaders need to abandon the three assumptions stated earlier and at the same time seek less rigid, more creative combinations.[38] Many times organizations struggle because they consider too narrow a range of options. Second, a leader needs to feel comfortable with paradoxical action,[39] e.g., "Even though you don't think I trust you, I do and I will." While larger organizations, including churches, are supposedly more impersonal, through proper action and attention, a larger organization might become even more personal than a small one.

According to Gardner, "One of the most important prerequisites for trust in a leader is steadiness."[40] By *steadiness*, Gardner means predictability. Gardner also notes that another important element for establishing organizational trust is fairness: "fairness when the issues are being openly adjudicated but, equally important, fairness in the back room. . . . Nothing is more surely stabilizing than confidence that the leader is unshakably fair in public and in private."[41]

One of the unshakable principles of Scripture is that since we are expected to trust our Heavenly Father, who is indeed trustworthy, we indeed can and ought to trust others. When Jesus gives us the many keys to right living in His Sermon on the Mount, we are expected to respond as He desires because of our trust level in Him. We don't have to worry about our reputations or storing up treasures on earth because our trust is in our Heavenly Father who has promised to supply all our needs. Christian leaders need to possess an unshakable trust in the Lord, a vertical trust, if you will, before trust can be practiced on the horizontal level within the organization.

One of the great themes of the New Testament is that of unity among the body of Christ. Paul told the Philippians that if they wanted to encourage him, "then make my joy complete by being like-minded, having the same love, being one in spirit and purpose" (Philippians 2:2). Peter desired that Christians "live in harmony with one another." James tells us that fights and quarrels result among Christians because of covetousness, and because we ask with wrong motives—to spend on our own pleasures rather than on His purposes. The absence of these positive characteristics results, in part, because of the absence of trust at the vertical level and a corresponding lack of trust at the horizontal level. So, it appears that the Christian leader has to deal with the concept of trust in the theological sense after all.

Jesus instructed His followers that if anyone wanted to be the greatest (presumably some perceive leaders in this *greatest* category), then he had to become the least. He told them that if someone wanted to be first (presumably some perceive leaders to be in this *first* category), then he had to be last. A leader who exhibits the positive characteristics outlined in 1 Corinthians 13 will have no trouble dealing with the paradox of organizational trust because such a leader will be trusted.

Regrettably, many Christian leaders who hold visible positions of leadership and who are active in a local church differentiate between what is expected of them in their personal walk with Christ and what is expected of them as Christian leaders in a corporate Christian context. In short, in our corporate expressions of Christianity we have neglected our corporate witness. We have said something to the effect that "it makes no difference that our corporate structures and the way we operate within them differ little from the typical secular corporate culture." The paradox is that Jesus strongly argued that people would be attracted to His cause because of the differences they would see in the corporate Christian community when compared with the secular world. This kind of bifurcation not only fails to produce trust in an organization, but further, the cause of the kingdom is significantly set back.

From this brief review, we see that the secular corporate world argues for high levels of trust in an organization. Trusting persons will be harder working people. Trusting persons will be more committed people. Trusting people will be more effective people. So it makes sense, after all, for the leader to manage and cultivate trust in an organization. And not only does it make good sense organizationally, but high levels of trust ought characterize the organization which calls itself Christian. This is particularly the case where power, authority, and leadership are involved.

Having set forth the conceptual discussion of leadership, power, authority, and trust, we now turn to some specific dimensions of leadership in the context of organizational concerns.

PART TWO

ORGANIZATIONAL DIMENSIONS OF LEADERSHIP

"It is not always a simple task to guide people who, though godly, have strong opinions of their own. The leader must not ruthlessly assert his will."

J. OSWALD SANDERS

"In the conventional mode people want to know whether the followers believe in the leader; a more searching question is whether the leader believes in the followers."

JOHN W. GARDNER

The heart of leadership rests not in conceptual formulations nor in theoretical analysis. Rather, the essential parts of leadership are most frequently observed in the actual practices of both leaders and followers within the context of organizations.

Some might consider this part of the book to be an attempt to develop an organizational theology of leadership. This is not intended. Others have already expended solid efforts in that direction. Alternatively, the focus of this section is to present and discuss this issue: what might obedience to the commands of Christ look like in organizational practice?

For example, how might the concepts of forgiveness and confrontation be practiced organizationally? What about matters such as excellence, fund-raising, and organizational growth? How do people within the organization both lead and follow?

CHOSEN BY GOD

Elsewhere in this book we have identified some of the tasks of leadership. In various places each of those tasks are reflected in a biblical example. In addition to being aware of the tasks of leadership, leaders who are effective are certain of the call of leadership.

It is a popular myth that those who hold leadership positions have eagerly aspired to those positions, are experiencing life on easy street, and because of the good life provided, want to hang on to the position for as long as possible. While one can always point to an example or two in support of this myth, my conversations with leaders, coupled with my experience, would suggest a totally different picture as follows: while persons in leadership are at peace with their current calling, they neither need it for purposes of ego nor desire it for reasons of security; in fact, most could eagerly identify another role responsibility in which they could function well. Simply put, leaders are in the positions they hold only because they believe they have been chosen by God. A leader in a Christian organization who doesn't sense that certain call of God may end up being a very frustrated leader. Why is it important to have this sense of calling?

While there are, to be sure, certain benefits, such as compensation, to given leadership positions, there are also a variety of detriments, including financial. Several examples of detriments might be helpful. First, every constituent believes he has a right to your time. As the leader of the organization, the CEO serves *all* the people. And it's not uncommon, given the consumer orientation that has pervaded the marketplace, for the employee, or parishioner, or the board member to ask, "What's in this for me?" Who else is better qualified to address this concern than the leader? In a Christian college setting, a variety of constituencies must be represented, and sometimes there is little similarity to demands raised. The faculty doesn't want what the students want. The alumni don't always want what the trustees desire. The supporting church has different expectations than does the community where the college is located. The parents sometimes are at odds with the administration. And the contributors believe that their voice should be a prominent one.

Second, the leader's family priorities are constantly in danger. The leader must fight carefully but persistently so that these family priorities are not placed in jeopardy. It is not unusual, even in Christian circles, to hear about such problems as marriages falling apart or children in open rebellion. Many leaders, therefore, are extremely time sensitive because time is perhaps the leader's most important asset and it must be carefully guarded.

Third, leaders by virtue of their positions of responsibility, and because of the always pressing time constraints, tend not to have many close friends with whom they can play or pray. The job of a leader is many times a lonely position. To be sure, leaders have many friends but seldom are they close friends.

A fourth detriment is financial. For example, while I know of few such surveys, the net worth of many non-leaders in the organization often exceeds the net worth of the leader. Why, given the fact that many leaders are the most highly paid in the organization? A key reason is that, while salaries tend to be larger than others within the organization, many CEOs and pastors are required, as part of the job, to live in organization-owned housing. As a result, and unlike non-leaders, they tend to build no equity. And, given past relatively high inflation rates, home equity has been a major factor in building net worth.

A fifth detriment is the nature of the work. As a former CEO has put it, "The buck stops here." And there is a price to be paid for buck-passing. Every leader knows that power is necessary to achieve organizational goals. Few leaders relish its use, particularly when personnel matters must necessarily be dealt with or when budgets must be adjusted—both high-stress situations. While to be sure there are some glamorous sides to leadership, the other side is also essential. The point to be made here is not to stay out of positions of leadership. Rather, the point is that leadership is a fairly high-priced calling and persons are advised not to rush headlong into it unless, after counting the costs, they are persuaded that God has still called them into such a position. Perhaps the attitude should be one of a reluctant but willing servant.

In Oswald Sanders' book, *Spiritual Leadership*, he notes the following:

> True greatness, true leadership, is achieved not by reducing men to one's service but in giving oneself in selfless service to them. And *that is never done without cost.* It involves drinking a bitter cup and experiencing a painful baptism of suffering. The true spiritual leader is concerned infinitely more with the service he can render God and his fellow men than with the benefits and pleasures he can extract from life. He aims to put more into life than he takes out of it.[1]

Here then is our first point—*leaders must have a clear sense of being chosen by God.*

The theology of being chosen by God is a rich one in Scripture. For example, Christ Himself told His followers:

> You did not choose me, but I chose you to go and bear fruit—fruit that will last. Then the Father will give you whatever you ask in my name (John 15:16).

Further, throughout the pages of the Old Testament, we see God vigorously at work choosing His leaders based a significant number of times on qualities other than human merit. The *call of Abram* is reflected in Genesis 12:1-3:

> Leave your country, your people, and your father's household and go to the land I will show you. I will make you into a great nation and I will bless you; I will make your name great, and you will be a blessing. I will bless those who bless you and whoever curses you I will curse; and all of the

peoples on earth will be blessed through you.

In these verses we don't see Abram trying to curry favor with God so that God would bless him. Rather, we see him content in his circumstances until the call of God came. The call of God clearly caused some discomfort as subsequent chapters of Genesis indicate—it meant leaving behind family and friends, constant moving, and the incredible demand that Abram sacrifice his only son. Even though the tradition of the times indicated that Esau was to be the son of blessing, *God had chosen Jacob.* God made His presence known to Jacob in a variety of ways, but the dream at Bethel bears noting:

> I am the Lord, the God of your father Abraham and the God of Isaac. I will give you and your descendants the land. . . . All peoples on earth will be blessed through you and your offspring. I am with you and will watch over you wherever you go, and I will bring you back to this land. I will not leave you until I have done what I have promised you (Genesis 28:13-15).

Later, after a heavenly wrestling match, God renamed His chosen servant Israel.

God revealed to *Joseph,* one of Jacob's sons, that he would one day hold a position of leadership. He was a bit outspoken about it, which made his already hateful brothers more hateful. Indeed, Joseph's path toward leadership included some rather distasteful elements.

Moses, former heir apparent to the throne of Pharaoh and erstwhile nomad shepherd was *called by God* through a burning bush: "When the Lord saw that he had gone over to look, God called to him from within the bush, 'Moses, Moses!' And Moses said, 'Here I am' " (Exodus 3:4). In the verses which follow, we discover that Moses was not immediately a willing leader. He used almost every trick in the book to argue that, in essence, God could have and should have made a better choice. Even after Moses had led the Children of Israel for some time, he still saw God, not himself, as the leader. In essence, he was suggesting that when the people complained to him, they were filing a complaint against God's ability to deliver and provide:

And in the morning you will see the glory of the Lord, because he has heard your grumbling against him. Who are we [Aaron and I], that you should grumble against us? (Exodus 16:7)

So they quarreled with Moses and said, "Give us water to drink." Moses replied, "Why do you quarrel with me? Why do you put the Lord to the test? (Exodus 17:2)

God's call of Joshua is recorded in Joshua 1:1-2, 6:

After the death of Moses the servant of the Lord, the Lord said to Joshua son of Nun, Moses' aide: "Moses my servant is dead. Now then, you and all these people, get ready to cross the Jordan River into the land I am about to give them—to the Israelites. . . . Be strong and courageous because you will lead these people to inherit the land."

After Joshua went off the scene, a leadership vacuum ensued in Israel, during which the judges—men and women *raised up by God*—played a significant role. Finally, the people wanted a king like the other nations. When Samuel went to the Lord to inquire, the Lord in essence said, "Well, it's not what I think is best, but I guess I'll give them a king." No resumes were solicited, no ads placed, for *God had already chosen His man, Saul:* "Then Samuel took a flask of oil and poured it on Saul's head and kissed him, saying, 'Has not the Lord anointed you leader over his inheritance?'" (1 Samuel 10:1)

The story of how *God chose David* is another fascinating account of how God selects leaders. Saul, because of continued disobedience to the commands of God, forfeited further opportunity to lead. On hearing this news, Samuel was somewhat downcast, which grieved God:

The Lord said to Samuel, "How long will you mourn for Saul, since I have rejected him as king over Israel? Fill your horn with oil and be on your way; I am sending you to Jesse of Bethlehem. I have chosen one of his sons to be king (1 Samuel 16:1).

When Samuel arrived at Jesse's house he just knew he would

be able to pick God's choice. But Samuel was wrong, and God said:

> Do not consider his appearance or his height, for I have rejected him. The Lord does not look at the things man looks at. Man looks at the outward appearance, but the Lord looks at the heart (1 Samuel 16:7).

Even Jesse had the wrong perspective. At last, Samuel pressed Jesse: "Are these all the sons you have?" When Jesse remarked that the youngest, David, was out tending sheep, the inference was, "You want him? You've got to be kidding!" But as soon as Samuel saw David, he heard from the Lord: "Rise and anoint him; he is the one" (v. 12).

If one has indeed been chosen by God, what limits if any does that selection suggest? If I am God's choice, does that mean I can serve for life? Surely the biblical examples just discussed might be interpreted by some to mean that. For example, the family leadership trusts mentioned in chapter 1—trusts where key family members hold positions of power to the exclusion of non-family members—might argue that leadership assignments ought to continue until the current leader chooses to step aside.

However, I believe that the Scripture better supports the view that *leaders ought to view their leadership assignment as stewardship of a temporary trust from the Lord rather than as something to be permanently clung to.* The pattern in Scripture seems to be that as long as the leader obeyed the will of the Lord, God was prepared to use that person. As noted earlier, Saul lost his position of leadership because of his disobedience.

From everything we read about Moses, he too was diligent in his service for God: "Since then no prophet has risen in Israel like Moses, whom the Lord knew face to face" (Deuteronomy 34:10). Yet, in spite of Moses' outstanding record, in spite of the fact that he faithfully took care of the people while they wandered in the desert for forty years, God told him that he wasn't going to be able to go into the Promised Land:

> Then Moses went out and spoke these words to all Israel: "I am now a hundred and twenty years old and I am no longer able to lead you. The Lord has said to me, 'You shall not

cross the Jordan'" (Deuteronomy 31:1-2).

Why then was Moses not permitted to lead the people into the Promised Land? Was it because he was no longer in good health? No, Moses was in incredibly good health when he died: "Moses was a hundred and twenty years old when he died, yet his eyes were not weak nor his strength gone" (Deuteronomy 34:7).

Why did God deprive him of the opportunity to lead? God answers:

> There on the mountain that you have climbed you will die and be gathered to your people, just as your brother Aaron died. . . . This is because both of you broke faith with me in the presence of the Israelites at the waters of Meribah Kadesh in the desert of Zin and because you did not uphold my holiness among the Israelites (Deuteronomy 32:50-51).

Just what did Moses do at Meribah Kadesh that disqualified him for leadership? God told Moses to speak to the rock so water would come forth; instead, Moses struck the rock (Numbers 20). To the average reader, this hardly seems like an offense that warrants so harsh a sanction, especially since God had told Moses on an earlier occasion to strike a rock for needed water (Exodus 17:5-7). Yet this time because Moses did not obey the exact command, God saw it as breaking faith with Him and as not upholding His holiness.

Without question, this episode sets a very high standard for God-chosen leaders. From it, we learn the following:

1. *Leaders chosen by God have an incredibly high standard to meet, and that standard is set by God.* The standard includes obedience and a concern for holy living.

2. *Leaders chosen by God should not assume that they will always be leaders.* Rather, a leader may remain in a position of leadership for a long period of time, but such longevity should result from the ongoing confirmation of God's Spirit, not from planned permanence from the beginning.

3. *Leaders chosen by God may not immediately experience the consequences of disobeying His standards.* In Moses' case, his sin occurred years prior to the time when God punished him for his lack of accountability. It's also important to note here that

Moses' sin was not one that in all probability would get him fired from a leadership position today. He hadn't had an affair with anybody, didn't get drunk, didn't kill anybody. Yet the standard that he violated was a standard important to God. It ultimately cost him his job, his retirement location, and his life—all in all, a pretty steep price for failing a leadership assignment.

4. *Leaders chosen by God ought to think about longer-term commitments in the positions God has placed them.* Too many times, as has been noted elsewhere, leaders of Christian organizations play the leadership musical chair game. "I need to get to the bigger church so that I get noticed by headquarters." In the Christian college movement it goes like this: "Well, I'll take the presidency here, stay a couple of years, and then see what opens up elsewhere." This could be translated to mean, "I really wish I were at a more famous, bigger school, and the first chance I get to make such a move, I'm gone." Perhaps the examples cited earlier suggest that this "promotion-by-moving" mentality needs to be reexamined.

Interestingly, those who observe Japanese business leaders note that one of the fundamental differences of Japanese companies, when compared with U.S. companies, is that the Japanese seem more committed to the long haul. In other words, American leaders have a tendency to opt for the quick bottom line. Their Japanese counterparts take the longer view. The leader who plans to be at the college or the church or the other organization for only five years and who is committed to bigger and better things may have a tendency to strive for the quick fix in order to get the impressive results that will make him or her more hirable at a bigger and better place. Interestingly, my study of Christian organizations, particularly Christian colleges, suggests that few "great" Christian colleges did not have at some point in their history a leader who committed himself or herself to remain there for a long period of time. While long tenure in a position is no guarantee of great achievement, there seems to be no great achievement without someone having made the commitment to long tenure.

Leaders chosen by God would also do well to remember that just because God has chosen them for a task does not, in and of itself, mean that the people to be led will automatically be followers. Indeed, Scripture mentions several accounts where the leaders went to some length to give evidence to the people of their God-given calling. (Perhaps we need to return to this standard.) Note the following two examples.

In the case of Moses, he was very concerned about the fact that his being "chosen by God" might not be convincing to some skeptics who would challenge his leadership: "What if they do not believe me or listen to me and say, 'The Lord did not appear to you'?" (Exodus 4:1) And God gave Moses signs of assurance to show that he was indeed divinely chosen.

Perhaps one of the most apprehensive times a new leader faces is when he or she stands in front of the people to be led for the first time. Dozens of questions must be going through his or her mind, including "Will they accept my leadership? Will they be subordinates only or will they be followers?" Moses too faced these concerns. So, when he finally stood before the people for the first time, he did not simply say, "God has chosen me to be your leader; let's get going." Instead he told them the story of his having been chosen by God and the evidences or signs for that choosing:

> Moses and Aaron brought together all the elders of the Israelites, and Aaron told them everything the Lord had said to Moses. He also performed the signs before the people, and they believed. And when they heard that the Lord was concerned about them and had seen their misery, they bowed down and worshiped (Exodus 4:29-31).

It is probably a fair rendering of "and they believed" that the people accepted Moses' leadership. Moses was concerned that the people see him as God's choice for leadership. So too must today's leaders.

The second biblical example is that of Nehemiah. As a holder of a significant appointment in the kingdom of Artaxerxes, some might have said he was on easy street. Yet when he had opportunity to inquire about his native people, the Jews, and their status in Jerusalem, he was given a very discouraging and troubling report. To say the least, he was quite discouraged: "When I heard these things, I sat down and wept. For some days I mourned and fasted and prayed before the God of heaven" (Nehemiah 1:4). But what could he do? After all, he was merely a cupbearer.

Presumably, it was during this time of aloneness with God that he received heavenly direction to proceed with the task of rebuilding the wall. As the story continued, he told the king about the problem and the king responded positively (Nehemiah 2:8). So Nehemiah returned to Jerusalem. It's important to note that, thus far, the leadership vision was just between God and Nehemiah: "I had not told anyone with me what God had put in my heart to do for Jerusalem" (Nehemiah 2:12).

After Nehemiah had examined the walls and had a good sense of the work that needed to be done, he called together the city "officials" and shared his possible dream. Then he added these curious words: "I also told them about the gracious hand of my God upon me and what the king had said to me" (Nehemiah 2:18). Again the picture is this: God gives the leader the vision; the leader ascertains the facts; he then involves the relevant parties who will be involved in carrying out the leadership vision; he shares with these people his sense of God's call and also the king's response; and then the leader waits for the people to respond.

As was the case of the people with Moses, the people here responded similarly: "Let us start rebuilding." It is doubtful that Nehemiah could have done this project by himself. He needed others to help with the work and he waited for their response before the work was begun. Again, we see that being chosen by God for a task does not insulate leaders from the responsibility of informing and consulting with the people.

Many Christian leaders are hesitant to share their vision with the people. They believe that the vision belongs to them and that if those being led hear the vision they will try to change it or adjust it—somehow make it less godly. This concern, however, does not appear to be a concern of Scripture. To further compound the picture, while we would like to believe that the people consulted by Moses and Nehemiah were godly persons, we don't even have that assurance. Both of these passages merely suggest that a God-given vision can be shared with the people, and furthermore, when such is done, the people will respond positively. What happens when they don't?

Then tough questions must be asked. Is the vision really of God or is it merely my own? Are the people so "backslidden" that they are incapable of responding to God's truth? Honest answers to these questions will help the leader know what to do next.

One final thought to be considered: leaders chosen by God have no option to be disobedient to the commands of Scripture. Such commands still apply. For example, when I see a verse such as Romans 12:10—"Be devoted to one another in brotherly love. Honor one another above yourselves"—I can't read into it an exception clause such as: "Because I am a leader I can ignore that concept." Many leaders translate *chosen by God* to mean "I am entitled to privileged status, and I don't have to adhere to all the other guidelines for Christian living found in the Beatitudes and elsewhere in Scripture." Indeed, the leader chosen by God has a tremendous responsibility to model the commands of Christ in every way.

THE BURDEN OF LEADERSHIP

In chapter 3 we observed that one ought not be in a position of leadership without a clear sense from the Lord that he or she is God's choice for the position. The burdens are too great and the stress too significant. If the leader is performing leadership functions, then the question must be asked: just what are the burdens of leadership and whose responsibilities are they?

This issue was squarely faced by Moses in Numbers 11. It seems that the exodus from Egypt was certainly nothing to write home about. Even though the people were initially delighted to leave the land of bondage, they soon began to compare their enslaved lives in Egypt with their nomadic existence in the desert. They had complained about food so the Lord provided manna. Indeed, it must have seemed to the leader, Moses, that all the people found time to do was complain:

> Now the people complained about their hardships in the hearing of the Lord, and when he heard them his anger was aroused. Then fire from the Lord burned among them and consumed some of the outskirts of the camp. When the people cried out to Moses, he prayed to the Lord and the fire died down. So that place was called Taberah, because fire from the Lord had burned among them.
>
> The rabble with them began to crave other food, and again the Israelites started wailing and said, "If only we had

meat to eat! We remember the fish we ate in Egypt at no cost—also the cucumbers, melons, leeks, onions and garlic. But now we have lost our appetite; we never see anything but this manna!" The manna was like coriander seed and looked like resin. The people went around gathering it, and then ground it in a handmill or crushed it in a mortar. They cooked it in a pot or made it into cakes. And it tasted like something made with olive oil (Numbers 11:1-8).

Further, the complaining was not just an isolated event, for the Scripture states that "Moses heard the people of *every* family wailing, each at the entrance to his tent" (Numbers 11:10).

Knowing they don't have the ability to meet every "need" presented to them, few things discourage leaders more than being constantly reminded of all that the organization ought to be doing but is not. This is particularly the case since words of praise or appreciation are infrequently shared with the leader. Note here that I'm not arguing that people ought not make ongoing suggestions for improvement. Such is critically important for the organization. Indeed, organizational satisfaction and the quest for excellence may be mutually exclusive concepts.

Lawrence Miller, for example, has argued that: "Satisfaction and excellence are inherently in conflict. Satisfaction implies acceptance of things as they are. Dissatisfaction is the source of motivation. It leads to actions to change that which is the source of discomfort. The achievement of excellence can occur only if the organization promotes a culture of creative dissatisfaction."[1] According to John Stott, without this kind of creative dissatisfaction, there may not be any organizational vision:

> So what is vision? It is an act of seeing, of course, an imaginative perception of things, combining insight and foresight. But more particularly, in the sense in which I am using the word, *it is compounded by a deep dissatisfaction with what is and a clear grasp of what could be. It begins with indignation over the status quo, and it grows into the earnest quest for an alternative.*[2]

Leaders, then, ought to value expressions of creative dissatisfaction or positive complaining. The Israelites, however, were not involved with the expression of either creative dissatisfaction or positive complaining. Indeed, their complaining had a devastating effect on Moses. He told God, in fact, that if He didn't have a better idea, he wanted to be put to death.

He expressed his frustration to the Lord this way:

> Why have you brought this trouble on your servant? What have I done to displease you that you put the burden of all these people on me? Did I conceive all these people? Did I give them birth? Why do you tell me to carry them in my arms, as a nurse carries an infant, to the land you promised on oath to their forefathers? Where can I get meat for all these people? They keep wailing to me, "Give us meat to eat!" I cannot carry all these people by myself; the *burden* is too heavy for me. If this is how you are going to treat me, put me to death right now—if I have found favor in your eyes—and do not let me face my own ruin (Numbers 11:11-15, italics added).

Leaders today ask the very same questions. "Lord, why did You bring me to this place? Lord, how come I did not know everything that was wrong with this place when I said yes to Your call? Lord, I want to be someplace else, someplace better—and someplace that doesn't have these kinds of problems." God must smile sometimes as He sees us go through periods like these. He knows, as do we, that He's in the business of delivering us *in* our circumstances, not *from* them. He wants us to remember His words to Israel:

> But now, this is what the Lord says—he who created you, O Jacob, he who formed you, O Israel: "Fear not, for I have redeemed you; I have called you by name; you are mine. *When* you pass through the waters, I will be with you; and *when* you pass through the rivers, they will not sweep over you" (Isaiah 43:1-2, italics added).

His answer now is the same as His answer to Moses then: "Is the Lord's arm too short? You will now see whether or not what I say will come true for you" (Numbers 11:23). Just what did He do for

Moses? How did He deal with Moses' burden?

God responded in two ways. First, He agreed to a plan of dispersed leadership (a concept discussed in chapter 1 of this book) by changing the organizational flowchart:

> The Lord said to Moses: "Bring me seventy of Israel's elders who are known to you as leaders and officials among the people. Have them come to the Tent of Meeting, that they may stand there with you. I will come down and speak with you there, and I will take of the Spirit that is on you and put the Spirit on them. They will help you carry the burden of the people so that you will not have to carry it alone" (Numbers 11:16-17).

In essence, God identified other persons who could help Moses, the leader, carry the load.

The question I ponder is why didn't Moses ask for help before? We don't know the answer, of course, but Moses may have been reluctant to share the burden of leadership. Furthermore, he may have been reluctant to delegate. God's answer to Moses' complaint suggests that dispersed leadership is appropriate, and it presupposes that the leader will delegate authority to others. Again, some leaders are reluctant to do this, but note, this was part of the divine answer for Moses.

There's a point to all this that the leader must not miss. The burden given to Moses was in essence God's burden. We don't get the picture here of God saying, "Well, now that I've made you the leader, good luck. Make sure the annual report is in on time." No, we get a picture of a God who identifies with the leader's frustration and burden and who does something about it.

Other Scripture also bears out this idea of a God who is actively monitoring the burdens carried by His people. In the Book of Job, for example, God set limits on what burdens Satan could throw at the patriarch. In Paul's letter to the Corinthians, he assured his readers that God was very much aware of their tolerance limits regarding the matter of temptation:

> No temptation has seized you except what is common to man. And God is faithful; he will not let you be tempted beyond what you can bear. But when you are tempted, he

will also provide a way out so that you can stand up under it (1 Corinthians 10:13).

And in Exodus 13, we see God selecting the route for the exodus from Egypt based primarily on His knowledge that the people could not handle the burdens of a shorter, more direct route:

When Pharaoh let the people go, God did not lead them on the road through the Philistine country, though that was shorter. For God said, "If they face war, they might change their minds and return to Egypt." So God led the people around by the desert road toward the Red Sea. The Israelites went up out of Egypt armed for battle (Exodus 13:17-18).

The second way God responded to Moses' plea regarding his burden was by providing a tangible answer to a tangible need. The people clamored for meat and God provided meat. God still is in the business of responding to tangible needs. Numerous Christian leaders could testify as to how God has tangibly met the needs of their organizations. I count myself among them.

To summarize this section, we see that the organizational burden is not solely the leader's; it's also the Lord's. We see that the solution for carrying the burden might include institutional reorganization, delegation (the leader *must* be willing and is expected to share the burden with others), and greater attention to dispersed leadership. And we see that God may respond directly to the need which triggered the "complaint" in the first place.

Our discussion thus far has focused on the general types of organizational burdens associated with leadership. But other burdens need to be discussed, namely the burden on the leader when the people go wrong and the burden on the people when the leader goes wrong. Each will be discussed in turn.

WHEN THE PEOPLE GO WRONG

We see clearly from Scripture that *the leader has the burden of developing an organizational response when the people go wrong.* Several examples will prove useful. A variety of chapters in the Book of Numbers discuss Moses' time with God on Mount Sinai. When he returned to the plain, he saw "the calf and the dancing" of the people. His response was not a mild, "Oh well, boys will be boys. I hope they get their act together." Rather, "his anger burned and he threw the tablets out of his hands, breaking them to pieces at the foot of the mountain" (Exodus 32:19). In brief, he was furious. And as their leader, he took it upon himself to see that sin was punished and fellowship restored with the holy God.

Leaders have a tendency to be soft on organizational sin. We don't call sin for what it is and sometimes protest that it's difficult to identify disobedience. Not so with Moses, who responded immediately to a clear violation of a God-given commandment. Charles Colson observes what we already know: "But all sin is an offense against God; to me, the miracle is that He has not already brought judgment on us all for the apostasy of our times."[3]

Moses, however, did more than simply express outrage for the sin of the people. He personally involved himself with administering various kinds of judgments and discipline. His reason for discipline had not only a personal dimension, but an organizational purpose. Because "the people were running wild" and "Aaron had let them get out of control," the people, and everything the people stood for, including their relationship to God, "became a laughingstock to their enemies" (Exodus 32:25). The reputation of the organization worthy of the name "Christian" was placed in jeopardy. It appears, then, that Moses' action was both personal and corporate, that is, targeted toward addressing individual actions and aimed at restoring the group's reputation for holiness to a pagan yet watching world.

Moses was still not finished. In addition to expressing outrage and administering judgment for both individual and corporate sin, he then went before God to "make atonement for . . . sin" (Exodus 32:30). To say that he took the failure of the people personally is understatement. He put not only his position as leader on the line, he put his life there as well:

> So Moses went back to the Lord and said, "Oh, what a great sin these people have committed! They have made themselves gods of gold. But now, please forgive their sin—but if not, then blot me out of the book you have written" (Exodus 32:31-32).

In addition to this example from the life of Moses, a similar illustration is taken from the life of Nehemiah, cupbearer for King Artaxerxes. While performing his duties at court, he was told of the great "trouble and disgrace" faced by the Jewish exiles back in Jerusalem. This soon-to-be governor of the people immediately took upon himself the burden of their welfare. He wept, mourned, fasted, and then prayed before the God of heaven:

> O Lord, God of heaven, the great and awesome God, who keeps his covenant of love with those who love him and obey his commands, let your ear be attentive and your eyes open to hear the prayer your servant is praying before you day and night for your servants, the people of Israel. I confess the sins we Israelites, including myself and my father's house, have committed against you. We have acted very wickedly toward you. We have not obeyed the commands, decrees, and laws you gave your servant Moses.
>
> Remember the instruction you gave your servant Moses, saying, "If you are unfaithful, I will scatter you among the nations, but if you return to me and obey my commands, then even if your exiled people are at the farthest horizon, I will gather them from there and bring them to the place I have chosen as a dwelling for my Name."
>
> They are your servants and your people, whom you redeemed by your great strength and your mighty hand. O Lord, let your ear be attentive to the prayer of this your servant and to the prayer of your servants who delight in revering your name. Give your servant success today by granting him favor in the presence of this man (Nehemiah 1:5-11).

As with Moses, Nehemiah's prayer included confession for the sin of the people. As with Moses, Nehemiah got personally involved attempting to correct the situation. For example, because some of the men had married women from pagan nations, Nehemiah "rebuked them and called curses down on them. I beat some of the men and pulled out their hair" (Nehemiah 13:25).

WHEN THE LEADER GOES WRONG
In addition to the burden on the leader when the people go wrong, *there is the burden on the people when the leader goes wrong.* The

Book of 2 Kings, for instance, is filled with example after example of this. When a godly king was on the throne, the people responded with godly responses. When an ungodly king was on the throne, the people were led to disobedience and God's judgment. These examples seem to suggest that a relationship exists between what happens to the people being led and the spiritual qualities which characterize the leader. Because of this seeming connection, the leader's spiritual maturity needs to be given much higher priority by leader search committees.

Another example of the failure of leadership and the concomitant negative burden it created for the people is found in Numbers 13. God wanted the Promised Land explored: "So at the Lord's command Moses sent them out from the desert of Paran. *All of them were leaders* of the Israelites" (Numbers 13:3, italics added). When these twelve leaders returned, each having seen the identical things, and each having heard God's promises that He would give the people the land, they nevertheless gave a divided report. Ten of them saw only the obstacles and said the job couldn't be done. The other two took the position that though obstacles were present, God was adequate to the task.

Unfortunately, the ten negative leaders were most persuasive with the people. "And they spread among the Israelites a bad report about the land they had explored" (Numbers 13:32). And how did the people respond? "We should choose a leader and go back to Egypt" (Numbers 14:4). They even threatened to stone Moses, Aaron, Joshua, and Caleb (v. 10).

The Lord saw the people's disobedience as an offense against Him and was deeply grieved and angered:

> The Lord said to Moses, "How long will these people treat me with contempt? How long will they refuse to believe in me, in spite of all the miraculous signs I have performed among them?
>
> "How long will this wicked community grumble against me? I have heard the complaints of these grumbling Israelites. So tell them, 'As surely as I live, declares the Lord, I will do to you the very things I heard you say: In this desert your bodies will fall—every one of you twenty years old or more who was counted in the census and who has grumbled against me. Not one of you will enter the land I swore with

uplifted hand to make your home, except Caleb son of Juphunneh and Joshua son of Nun. As for your children that you said would be taken as plunder, I will bring them in to enjoy the land you have rejected. But you—your bodies will fall in this desert. Your children will be shepherds here for forty years, suffering for your unfaithfulness, until the last of your bodies lies in the desert. For forty years—one year for each of the forty days you explored the land—you will suffer for your sins and know what it is like to have me against you.' I the Lord have spoken, and I will surely do these things to this whole wicked community, which has banded together against me. They will meet their end in this desert; here they will die" (Numbers 14:11, 27-35).

Simply put, these people paid dearly for the sinful disobedience of their leaders. Here then is another reason for the followers to insist on accountability from their leaders. When the leader fails, the burden many times falls on the people. In the area of failed leadership there are no such things as victimless sins.

THE ART OF CARRYING BURDENS

The desire to have a burden-free existence is noble but, at the same time, naive. The record of Scripture constantly presents examples of leaders with burdens of various kinds. Alternatively, from Adam to Abraham, from David to Daniel, we see a God who is constantly at work delivering people, not from their circumstances but in them. The burdens of leadership are no different. There is then no such thing as a burden-free life. The question then becomes, how do we cope?

First, we are told to cast our care on the Lord:

Young men, in the same way be submissive to those who are older. Clothe yourselves with humility toward one another, because, "God opposes the proud but gives grace to the humble." Humble yourselves, therefore, under God's mighty hand, that he may lift you up in due time. Cast all your anxiety on him because he cares for you (1 Peter 5:5-7).

We are told to commit our ways to the Lord: "Commit your way to the Lord; trust in him and he will do this" (Psalm 37:5). We are told to acknowledge Him in all our ways: "Trust in the Lord with all your heart and lean not on your own understanding; in all your ways acknowledge him, and he will make your paths straight" (Proverbs 3:5-6).

Assuming I have done this, then what? Several other suggestions are appropriate. First, we are to share our burdens with others: "Carry each other's burdens, and in this way you will fulfill the law of Christ" (Galatians 6:2). I can't have another bear my burden if I don't share it, and not very many leaders are good sharers of burdens. Why? Probably one reason is that they have gotten "burned" for having done so. A second is that leaders are not to carry burdens that they ought not deal with in the first place.

Many leaders, for instance, "carry the world on their shoulders" when all God wants them to do is carry only a small piece of it. Many leaders worry or carry "wrong" burdens when God wants them to carry "right" burdens. For example, note the following verses:

Do not be anxious about anything, but in everything, by prayer and petition, with thanksgiving, present your requests to God. And the peace of God, which transcends all understanding, will guard your hearts and your minds in Christ Jesus (Philippians 4:6-7).

Now I don't believe these verses tell me that I should be unconcerned or unburdened about a lost and dying world. I don't believe these verses tell me I should have no concern for my children or my wife. Paul, for example, lists his burdens in 2 Corinthians 11. After enumerating a long list, he notes the following additional one: "Besides everything else, I face daily the pressure of my concern for all the churches" (2 Corinthians 11:28). Many leaders could make similar statements.

I believe the point of the Philippians passage, then, is that we are to focus our concerns on the right burdens, burdens which God will help us carry, burdens such as those represented by the following verses:

And we pray this in order that you may live a life worthy of the Lord and may please him in every way; bearing fruit in every good work, growing in the knowledge of God (Colossians 1:10).

Finally, brothers, whatever is true, whatever is noble, whatever is right, whatever is pure, whatever is lovely, whatever is admirable—if anything is excellent or praiseworthy—think about such things (Philippians 4:8).

Set your minds on things above, not on earthly things (Colossians 3:2).

What kinds of concerns are we to avoid? Jesus gives us one such list recorded in Matthew 6:25-34:

Therefore I tell you, do not worry about your life, what you will eat or drink; or about your body, what you will wear. Is not life more important than food, and the body more important than clothes? Look at the birds of the air; they do not sow or reap or store away in barns, and yet your heavenly Father feeds them. Are you not much more valuable than they? Who of you by worrying can add a single hour to his life?

And why do you worry about clothes? See how the lilies of the field grow. They do not labor or spin. Yet I tell you that not even Solomon in all his splendor was dressed like one of these. If that is how God clothes the grass of the field, which is here today and tomorrow is thrown into the fire, will he not much more clothe you, O you of little faith? So do not worry saying, "What shall we eat?" or "What shall we drink?" or "What shall we wear?" For the pagans run after all these things, and your heavenly Father knows that you need them. But seek first his kingdom and his righteousness, and all these things will be given to you as well. Therefore do not worry about tomorrow, for tomorrow will worry about itself. Each day has enough trouble of its own.

In short, the list includes our lives (though it doesn't follow that we should be reckless or abuse our God-given temple), food and drink, and the kind of clothes we wear. We're also told not to worry about the burden of tomorrow. When we couple our faith in the power of Christ *with* the burden we carry, we practice conscientious Christian living. When we carry our burden *without* coupling it to faith in an all-powerful God, we'll end up being preoccupied with worry.

The exhortation "not to worry" in the Philippians passage follows with ways to make sure that we don't. First, we present our burdens to the Lord in prayer or petition. We give them to Him. Second, we wrap those petitions with praise or thanksgiving. When Hezekiah was faced with the burden of seemingly insurmountable odds militarily, he had no other option than to give the situation to God:

> And Hezekiah prayed to the Lord: "O Lord Almighty, God of Israel, enthroned between the cherubim, you alone are God over all the kingdoms of the earth. You have made heaven and earth. Give ear, O Lord, and hear; open your eyes, O Lord, and see; listen to all the words Sennacherib has sent to insult the living God.
>
> It is true, O Lord, that the Assyrian kings have laid waste all these peoples and their lands. They have thrown their gods into the fire and destroyed them, for they were not gods but only wood and stone, fashioned by human hands. Now, O Lord our God, deliver us from his hand, so that all kingdoms on earth may know that you alone, O Lord, are God" (Isaiah 37:15-20).

And God gave him a tremendous victory. Jehoshaphat faced similar adversity with similar results:

> Do not be afraid or discouraged because of this vast army. For the battle is not yours, but God's. . . . You will not have to fight this battle. Take up your positions; stand firm and see the deliverance the Lord will give you, O Judah and Jerusalem. Do not be afraid; do not be discouraged. Go out to face them tomorrow, and the Lord will be with you (2 Chronicles 20:15, 17).

Leaders often have no other option but to give their burden to the Lord. This is what God desires all along.

When we who are leaders give our burdens to the Lord, the Philippians passage suggests that we will experience the peace of

God, and further, that that peace will transcend all our understanding. And neither our hearts nor our minds will be preoccupied otherwise. Indeed, when burdens are given to Him, we can sigh with relief. This is the only way a leader can keep a "cool head," so to speak, during a particularly burdensome time.

Finally, and paradoxically, there seems to be a relationship between God's deliverance and the gravity of my burden. The more grave the situation, the more willing may be the leader to turn the burden over to Him, and hence the greater the praise and glory which goes to the Heavenly Father when victory results. In Judges 7, for example, Gideon was getting ready to go to battle against already incredible odds. But, incredibly, God seemed to think that the odds were not great enough: "The Lord said to Gideon, 'You have too many men for me to deliver Midian into their hands. [I do not want] Israel [to] boast against me that her own strength has saved her' " (Judges 7:2). God wanted the glory for the victory. He didn't want Israel to think that the victory was theirs. Clearly, God wanted both the burden *and* the glory. As leaders, we are tempted to give Him the burdens and then claim the glory. God wants both the burdens and the glory.

FOLLOWERSHIP

Most persons would agree that one of the characteristics of our society is that from an early age, we're taught to be followers. I well remember my childhood days in school and the teacher's constant reminders to make sure I followed the directions. One of the games we played during recess was "Follow the Leader." One of the marks of a good teacher in those days was to make sure young students knew how to make a line, stand in line, and follow whoever was at the head of the line—and to do all of this in an orderly fashion.

Thirty years later the emphasis on being a follower has become much more subtle if not totally nonexistent in our Christian culture. The focus of our efforts is on leadership. As Gardner notes: "We expect our leaders to be sensitive to and to serve the basic needs of our constituents, expect them to have faith in their constituents and a caring concern for them."[1]

Churches are seemingly forever offering seminars on leadership. Christian colleges proudly proclaim their positions as preparers of future leaders. And, indeed, prospective students make decisions about which college to attend based on the kind of leadership training they will receive. Even a current Christian periodical is entitled *Leadership*.

While I don't object to an emphasis on leadership, this emphasis has occurred at the expense of an equally valid emphasis on followership. (I would note that I have never seen any kind of conference on followership.) Yet, as Engstrom has observed: "What most of us need is more training in how to follow."[2]

Paradoxically, many who believe they are followers are in essence leaders. As has been noted elsewhere, it is rare that one is a leader in all dimensions of life or a follower in all dimensions of life. The reality is usually that, during any given week, one serves, alternatively, and in a variety of roles, as both leader and follower.

When Katz and Lazarsfeld were doing the research which was ultimately reported in their book, *Personal Influence*,[3] they attempted to locate opinion leaders. As might be expected, they found opinion leaders in official positions of responsibility. But they also found them in a variety of followership roles: "Unofficial leaders lead without benefit of authoritative office: here are the key men of a work gang, the sparkplugs of a salesman rally, the elder statesmen who sit on park benches talking for newspapers."[4] These opinion leaders, then, lead in their own way, perhaps not as a Churchill would, but they nonetheless still have followers.

The focus of this chapter deals with the subject of followership. Just what in the world is a follower? What are the responsibilities of followership? What are the privileges of followership? What ought to be the relationship of followers to leaders? Leaders to followers? And how shall we decide who to follow?

BIBLICAL PERSPECTIVES ON LEADERSHIP AND FOLLOWERSHIP

While there are those who raise legitimate concerns about whether or not the concept of leadership is anything more than an abstraction, the Scripture nevertheless discusses the subject and gives us models of both positive and negative leadership and followership. Following are some of the ways the Old Testament deals with the subject of leadership (italics added whenever the word *lead* appears):

> Now go, *lead* the people to the place I spoke of, and my angel will go before you (Exodus 32:34).

The concept of *lead* as used here suggests the taking of a group or the transporting of a group from one area to another, as in exile or as in colonization.

Another use of the word *lead* is found in Numbers 27:16-17:

> May the Lord, the God of the spirits of all mankind, appoint a man over this community to go out and come in before them, one who will *lead* them out and bring them in, so the Lord's people will not be like sheep without a shepherd.

Here the context suggests, among other things, the idea of carrying out, bringing out, escape. Also suggested is the idea of commanding or giving direction.

In Isaiah 49:10 another use of the word *lead* appears:

> They will neither hunger nor thirst, nor will the desert heat or the sun beat upon them. He who has compassion on them will guide them and *lead* them beside springs of water.

Here the word suggests strong affirmative action on the part of the leader. The one who leads does so by driving forth as one would drive an animal or chariot. It implies the follower is being impelled to do something.

It should be noted that thus far the words used for *lead* have focused more on what the one doing the leading does rather than on the leader himself. The usage in Deuteronomy 20:9 (KJV), however, focuses on the position of leader:

> And it shall be, when the officers have made an end of speaking unto the people, that they shall make captains of the armies to *lead* the people.

Here we see the leader as one who is the head or chief, the one who is first or in the forefront.

Another use of the word *lead* is found in Psalm 23:2:

> He makes me lie down in green pastures, he *leads* me beside quiet waters.

Here the word focuses once again on the function of leadership and suggests protection, sustenance, and guidance for those being led. Implicit in its use is the idea that one will lead gently.

To summarize this inexhaustive but illustrative survey of the

Old Testament portrayal of leadership, we see that while there is recognition of the leader as someone who is chief or first or foremost, the significant concern is for *how* the leading takes place. At times the one who leads needs to do so affirmatively. At other times the focus must be directional, as in helping those being led achieve a given destination. At other times the leader has a shepherd's role, where the welfare of those being led (i.e., care, food, protection, guidance) becomes the top priority. Leadership is defined more in the sense of what the leader will do for the people rather than on how the people will respond to the leader.

The New Testament also uses the word *lead* in a variety of ways. For example, when Jesus taught the disciples how to pray, He included the following words:

> And *lead* us not into temptation, but deliver us from the evil one (Matthew 6:13).

His use of the word *lead* here suggests bringing something or carrying something inward, in a protective sense.

Jesus used a different word for *lead* in Matthew 15:14:

> Leave them; they are blind guides. If a blind man *leads* a blind man, both will fall into a pit.

Lead in this instance is used in the sense of showing someone the way. The idea is of leading through teaching.

Yet another use of the word appears in Mark 13:11 (KJV):

> But when they shall *lead* you, and deliver you up, take no thought beforehand what ye shall speak.

In this context, *lead* is being used to mean "in a forceful or driving way."

Other New Testament texts indicate still other meanings, such as "to capture," "the passing of time," and "to take around as a companion." As with the Old Testament references, however, the New Testament focus pertains more to the function of leading than to the position of leader.

A further observation about leadership suggests that it is a multidimensional concept. There is no *one* leadership function. Rather, there may be several.

Interestingly, the Scriptures say far more about following than about leading—more than three times the number of references in comparison. What follows is a brief review of the ways the concept of followership is presented in both the Old and New Testaments (italics added whenever the word *follow* appears).

One Old Testament usage is in Deuteronomy 16:20:

> *Follow* justice and justice alone, so that you may live and possess the land the Lord your God is giving you.

The word *follow* here suggests an intensity of pursuit as of one pursuing a quarry. This is more than acquiescing to a leader or following from afar.

Exodus 11:8 reflects another use of the word:

> All these officials of yours will come to me, bowing down before me saying, "Go, you and all the people who *follow* you!" After that I will leave.

The idea here is that of walking along side of, and includes the idea of endurance.

In the New Testament, Acts 12:8 describes Peter's miraculous escape from prison.

> Then the angel said to him, "Put on your clothes and sandals." And Peter did so. "Wrap your cloak around you and *follow* me," the angel told him.

Here the meaning is "accompaniment," "to be in the same way with," "union." It implies clear direction as well as close proximity between the leader and follower. The same meaning is found in Jesus' words recorded in Matthew 8:22: "But Jesus told him, '*Follow* me, and let the dead bury their own dead.'"

Another use of *follow* appears in Matthew 4:19: "Come, *follow* me," Jesus said, "and I will make you fishers of men." Here, the context suggests physical presence, but not on equal footing. In short, I am to remain close to the leader, but I am clearly to remain behind because I'm not in charge—he is.

Mark 16:17 (KJV) reflects yet another use of the word *follow*:

> And these signs shall *follow* them that believe; In my name shall they cast out devils; they shall speak with new tongues.

The idea here is that of following near, knowing one fully, with the goal of conforming.

The Apostle Paul also gives us a look at what it means to follow:

> Not as though I had already attained, either were already perfect: but I *follow* after, if that I may apprehend that for which also I am apprehended of Christ Jesus (Philippians 3:12, KJV).

The idea here is one of pursuit, of pressing toward a particular goal.

A final New Testament reference, and yet another use of the word *follow*, is found in 2 Thessalonians 3:7:

> For you yourselves know how you ought to *follow* our example.

This time the context indicates imitation and/or modeling. Indeed, the Greek word used here is the one from which we get our word *mimic*.

Both the Old and New Testaments identify telling similarities between leadership and followership: (1) both leadership and followership can be intensive; (2) there need not be a gap between those leading and those following; and (3) leadership involves showing someone the way and teaching, while following involves attention to modeling. In the Old Testament we do see the concept of the leader as chief, though such is not suggested as the only model or even the best. Further, we see the prime function of the leader to be that of protector or guide. We also see the responsibility for the one who follows to do so closely, albeit from behind.

The overall picture we get from Scripture reflects several key considerations. First, it is difficult to discuss either followership or leadership without careful attention to both concepts. Without followers there can be no leaders. Without leaders there can be no followers. Each group depends on the other for its position or existence. As a result, the concepts of leader and follower tend to be complementary (also complimentary) rather than competitive.

Second, Scripture presents both concepts more as verbs than as nouns. Indeed, Scripture seems preoccupied with what leaders and followers do, as opposed to their name, rank, or status. Leaders, according to Scripture, have responsibilities that include guiding, sustaining, protecting, teaching, and shepherding. Followers have the responsibility for, among other things, submitting to (1 Peter 2:13ff), praying and interceding for (1 Timothy 2:1-2), and remaining close to leaders. Because of our culture's emphasis on leadership, however, many people, including Christians, find it much easier to be leaders than to be followers.

OTHER PERSPECTIVES ON FOLLOWERSHIP

Simply put, there is not an abundance of literature on following. John Gardner, along with Ted Engstrom and Ed Dayton have, however, provided some useful insights on this subject. In this section we'll first review Gardner's perceptions and then turn to those of others.

According to Gardner, "Leaders are almost never as much in charge as they are pictured to be, followers almost never are as submissive as one might imagine."[5] Further, and reflecting on the work of George Simmel (1858-1918), Gardner notes that "followers have about as much influence on their leaders as their leaders have on them. Leaders cannot maintain authority . . . unless followers are prepared to believe in that authority. In a sense, leadership is conferred by followers."[6] I find this comment absolutely fascinating because there are repeated examples in Scripture where it appears that the leader went to great lengths to present his leadership claims and his program for change to the people in order to legitimize his leadership. A careful study of how Moses was selected by God and how God prepared Moses to make his presentation to the people ("What will I do if the people don't believe me?") is but one illustration of this.

Gardner further argues that in large part the success or failure of the leader is dependent as much as, if not more, on the followers than on the leader: "Good constituents produce good leaders. They not only select good ones, they make them better by holding them to standards of performance."[7] Many times "leaders" assume that because they hold a given position, therefore, they are leaders. Not so, says Gardner:

> The assumption by line executives that, given their rank and authority, they can lead without being leaders is one reason bureaucracies stagnate. They are given subordinates, but they cannot be given a following. Surprisingly, many of them don't know they are not leading. They mistake the exercise of authority for leadership, and as long as they persist in that mistake they will never learn the art of turning subordinates into followers.[8]

What is it, then, that followers want from a leader? According to Gardner:

> Followers do like being treated with consideration, do like to have their say, do like a chance to exercise their own initiative—and participation does increase acceptance of decisions. But there are times when followers welcome rather than reject authority, want prompt and clear decisions from the leader, want to close ranks around the leader. The ablest and most effective leaders do not hold to a single style; they may be highly supportive in personal relations when that is needed, yet capable of a quick authoritative decision when the situation requires it.[9]

Additionally, followers desire "effective two-way communication," and significant face-to-face communication. As Gardner notes, "Wise leaders are continuously finding ways to say to their constituents, 'I hear you.' "[10] Furthermore, followers readily pick up and respond to nonverbal communication. According to Gardner, "Truly gifted leaders know not only what constituents need but what they fear, what they long to be, what they like best about themselves. Woodrow Wilson said, 'The ear of the leader must ring with the voices of the people.' "[11] Gardner also suggests that it's important for leaders to believe in their followers:

> In the conventional mode people want to know whether the followers believe in the leader; a more searching question is

whether the leader believes in the followers.[12]

Gardner's observations, interestingly enough, are consistent with the earlier observations from Scripture regarding leading and following.

One of the most powerful references to the leader's responsibility to his or her followers comes from the book, *The Art of Japanese Management*.[13] The authors reflect on the issue of power and leadership competence so as to ascertain just what is an effective leader. They note, for example, the cultural differences between leading/following roles in Japan as compared with the Western world:

> The prime qualification of a Japanese leader is his acceptance by the group, and only part of that acceptance is founded on his professional merits. The group's harmony and spirit are the main concern. Whereas in the West work group leaders tend to emphasize task and often neglect group maintenance activities, in Japan maintenance of a satisfied work group goes hand in hand with role.[14]

When asked, "What really makes for an effective leader?" their response is "followership." I here repeat a portion of a quote cited earlier:

> While the findings fill volumes, the consistent picture of the effective leader is one who adopts the style of a "superfollower," who serves with his followers' blessing and consent, and who is able to inspire because he is first able to respond to their needs and concerns.[15]

For the Christian leader, the concept of a *superfollower* is indeed a powerful one. It includes dealing with basic discipleship expectations:

- Do you want to be the greatest? You must be the least.
- Do you want to be first? You must learn to be last.
- Do you want to be served? You must learn to serve.
- Do you want to be a leader? You must learn to be a superfollower of those you lead.

To paraphrase John Yoder, leaders are to be followers not

because they are wonderful and generous persons, not because they are convinced that followership will yield the ultimate conquest of the people they lead, not because it reflects the best thinking of the current religious community regarding servant leadership, and not because higher profits or results will be achieved. Rather, leaders ought to be followers of the people they lead because Christ commands us to be followers—followers, first of all, of Himself and secondly, followers in the sense of putting the needs of those we lead before our own.[16]

FOLLOWERSHIP QUALITIES

Engstrom and Dayton identify nine followership qualities.

1. *Commitment.* "Our commitment is first to the person we work for, second to our fellow workers and third to the organization."[17]

2. *Understanding.* "We know the task, our role in it, how we relate to others, whom we will be working with, their style and goals, and a host of other data."[18]

3. *Loyalty.* "We will represent our leader fairly and carefully. We will protect his or her reputation."[19]

4. *Communication.* We have elsewhere discussed the need of the leader to communicate with followers. The focus here is the follower communicating with the leader and with others who work with that same leader. Complete information should be provided, rather than giving only what one might think the leader wants to hear.

5. *Competence.* "If you don't have what is needed to do a job, there is no way you can be a follower in that situation. . . . It's all right to stretch ourselves, but there are times when we have to say honestly and forthrightly, 'I don't think I can do that job adequately.' "[20] In my experience at a variety of institutions, rarely have I had persons admit to me that they did not possess the competence to do the job. Yet it had become clear to everyone, except the person involved, that such was lacking. When the person involved, in addition, is unwilling to grow or learn, the situation becomes even more difficult.

6. *Promise keeping.* "Good followers do what they say (promise) they will do. When they recognize that they are not going to be able to keep the promise to their leader or their teammates, they immediately let the others know."[21]

7. *Participation.* "Good followers understand where they fit in the larger whole. They recognize that a failure (to participate) on their part can jeopardize everyone else. That is why commitment to others beside the leader is so important."[22]

8. *Getting along.* This quality focuses not only on the importance of participation but also on *how* one participates with others. "Getting along means spending time with others when what they are doing may seem frivolous or unnecessary. . . . Getting along is recognizing that often our own feet seem to be made of clay and others have something to tell us. Getting along means *allowing* others to help us, compliment us and sometimes criticize us."[23]

9. *Sacrifice.* "We often talk about the cost of leadership. Seldom do we hear about the cost of followership—'take up his cross daily.' Following has about it a willingness to accept the possibility of our own execution. . . . It may be the execution of personal dreams and aspirations. It may be the execution of our own highly held opinions. It may be the offering up of our individualism for the good of the cause of which we are a part. . . . We discover that being a good follower calls for sacrifice we never imagined."[24]

THE FAILURES OF FOLLOWERS

The literature of Christendom is filled with accounts of leaders who failed. Given our earlier discussion, however, of the almost symbiotic relationship between leaders and followers, almost by definition, then, the failure of leaders must be in some way connected to the failure of followers. But, where is the literature on the failures of followers? As Gardner has observed:

> There is a vast literature on the failures of leadership—on the abuse of power, injustice, indecisiveness, shortsightedness, and so on. Who will write the essay on individual and collective failures among followers?[25]

Gardner then proceeds to identify three "failings of followers." First, he discusses the *failure of noninvolvement* such as "apathy, passivity, cynicism and habits of spectator-like noninvolvement which invite the abuse of power of leaders."[26] The concern here, of course, is that proper followership insists on leadership ac-

83

countability. If followers don't insist on accountability, it is more likely that the leader will abuse and/or misuse power.

A second failure of followers is to *"collaborate in their own self-deception."* As Gardner notes, "A citizenry that wants to be lied to will have liars as leaders."[27] This type of deception often takes place when followers are unwilling to face facts. In higher education, for example, few if any colleges are willing to admit that they are not committed to educational excellence. One of the most significant roles of accrediting associations is to challenge what in some cases is an institutional illusion or fantasy regarding its own situation. The ability to establish organizational goals, coupled with a hard organizational look at where an organization is compared to where it wants to be, is absolutely critical to proper planning. Such planning will not take place if self-deception is practiced by both leaders and followers.

A third failure of followers is *"the failure of group cohesion among the followers*—a circumstance that makes leadership very difficult indeed."[28]

Several other failures of followers besides those mentioned by Gardner should also be considered. For instance and simply stated, it's more "fun" to be a leader than a follower, or at least that's the perception of followers. As a result, more followers want to carry out following by trying to be leaders, thereby compounding the leader's plight. A quote from a recent *Chronicle of Higher Education* article illustrates this concern: "An ironic aspect of the weakened presidency is that people in higher education seem to want more leadership but are less willing to be 'followers.' "[29]

Another failure of followers is to overestimate the power possessed by leaders. A variety of followers regularly present themselves as supplicants in front of a leader's door expecting that, with a "wave of the hand" or with a "tersely worded command," a given problem will be resolved. Most leaders have far less power than imagined in the eyes of the followers, and leaders have a responsibility to let followers know the limits of the position they hold. As Engstrom has observed: "Leadership that is authentic and which builds Christian community must destroy the illusion that power resides in the person and office of the leader."[30]

Closely related to the preceding observation is the fact that followers sometimes properly insist on controls within the organization to prevent the abuse and/or misuse of power. These controls, if not carefully designed and implemented, may make leading both difficult and cumbersome. At the same time, notwithstanding these cumbersome organizational structures, the followers also have a tendency to blame the leader when things don't get done more quickly. Perhaps this failing could be categorized as the failure of unrealistic expectations.

WHEN DO WE STOP FOLLOWING?

Because every leader is a follower (leaders follow Christ and others within the organization; also, leaders in one organization may be followers in another, e.g., Rotary) and every follower a leader (I may be a follower at work, but a leader in my home, church, etc.), this question must be generally faced by all. When do I stop following the leader?

At first glance, the answer appears to be easy. Using our previous definitions, it would seem that one stops following when the leader stops leading. This answer, admittedly highly subjective, suggests that when the leader stops meeting the needs of the follower, following stops. While I, as a follower, may still be subordinate to a position of authority, the fact that I am a subordinate doesn't make me a follower. In essence, I can stop following, but still retain my position as a subordinate within the organization.

Another principled option I have, however, and one not readily chosen by those persons who stop following, particularly during times of economic tightness, is to leave the organization and go elsewhere. Perhaps this is the most honest option for the follower.

Furthermore, since leaders are also followers of people they lead, leaders ought also to have the option to stop following the people. If the people being led are absolutely opposed to the direction a given leader might suggest, then the leader must carefully evaluate future effectiveness in other areas as well.

Both leaders and followers must candidly admit that there are times when it is right for the followers to stop following and/or for the leader to stop leading. The ideal situation would be one where both affected leaders and followers would draw this conclusion on their own initiative without someone else drawing those conclusions for them. Occasionally followers must have the integrity to admit that they wholeheartedly disagree with a general but substantial organizational direction, and that they would be better off becoming a supportive subordinate or going elsewhere. What happens many times, however, is that when followers stop following and become unhappy subordinates, they do everything in their power to get rid of the current leader. But unless the leader is clearly violating some clearly stated biblical principle, this kind of personal organizational agenda may run afoul of Scripture.

If the follower cannot become either a contented subordinate or is not willing to work for change in a proper manner, then I would argue that such an individual should leave the organization and go somewhere else where the organizational agenda would be more compatible with his or her personal agenda.

So too for the leader. Leaders must be in step with their followers. An effective leader works hard at knowing the aspirations and goals of the people being led and tries to move the organization in that direction. Assuming the organizational goals are not violative of biblical principles, the leader needs to mesh the organizational goals, as expressed by the followers, with his or her own, hopefully, God-given, agenda. The leader who finds that the organization is unwilling to move toward group-identified goals or where his or her goals no longer fit the organization's desires ought also consider selecting another organization. In my view, it is wrong for a leader (in the absence of significant organizational deviation from biblical principles) to browbeat the followers for not performing up to the given agenda. Perhaps it's time for that leader to stop following and go elsewhere.

Engstrom and Dayton have stated their own pointed observations to the question, "When do we stop following?"

Our Western society is mobile not only where people live but in the commitments we make to a local church, a local community or the organization of which we may currently be a part. Sometimes no longer following is shaped by our culture. But are there other good reasons for abandoning a leader? Someone has said that the trust we place in our leaders is based on their competency and their motivation. If they are not competent to lead, we will no longer be able to follow. If their motivation is such that we no longer see them as following Christ, we should not be expected to continue to follow.

These words are more easily given than applied. Many causes fail because the leader no longer has followers. Pray much before you stop following![31]

Several additional observations from Scripture might be useful. First, contrary to popular belief, Scripture doesn't provide a lot of support to those who either don't like the leader and want to "dump him" or to those who want to "run away" from difficulty. Scripture instead gives us examples of those who learned to lead only after they had learned to follow. The cases of Jonah and Joseph are but two. One *tried to stop leading* because of the difficult task God assigned and the other *could have stopped following* God because of the terrible circumstances God "provided" for him as part of his leadership training.

In the case of Jonah, he was given a preaching assignment to share God's message of judgment with the people of Nineveh. Jonah thought about this leadership assignment and decided God had made a mistake. The leadership assignment was too difficult. So he decided to run and became part of a travel group to Tarshish. Many times this is a typical response of a leader to a difficult leadership assignment. Yet according to Psalm 139, one cannot run or hide from God:

> You know when I sit and when I rise; you perceive my thoughts from afar. You discern my going out and my lying down; you are familiar with all my ways. . . . Where can I go from your Spirit? Where can I flee from your presence? If I go up to the heavens, you are there; if I make my bed in the depths, you are there. If I rise on the wings of the dawn, if I settle on the far side of the sea, even there your hand will guide me, your right hand will hold me fast. If I say, "Surely the darkness will hide me and the light become night around me," even the darkness will not be dark to you; and the night will shine like the day, for darkness is as light to you (Psalm 139:2-3, 7-12).

Leaders know this, but try anyhow. God proceeded to get Jonah's attention (He usually does), and he became an effective if not ungrateful leader for the cause of the kingdom. The message is clear to leaders: it is difficult to outrun God by trying to escape a difficult leadership assignment.

In the case of Joseph, adversity could have caused him to stop following God during the Lord's preparation of him for a future leadership assignment. He was sold into slavery by his brothers; he was unfairly accused by an immoral woman and sentenced to prison; and his good deed to another was forgotten. Yet throughout such ill treatment, he was not bitter. Rather, he waited patiently until God, in His own time, opened the door for subsequent leadership opportunities. The message here is clear to followers preparing to be leaders: God's leadership boot camp always provides just the right preparation for future leadership assignments. And further, His timing is always perfect.

As difficult as it may sometimes seem, leaders need to keep leading and keep following.

CHAPTER
SIX

CONFRONTATION

One of the most important yet one of the most difficult assignments facing the leader is the task of confrontation—both of issues and of people. When one thinks about the concept of confrontation, a number of scenarios come to mind—labor versus management, parent versus child, country versus country. In spite of the difficulties involved with confrontation, leaders know that in order to be faithful both to the responsibilities of the position and to the commands of Scripture, the leadership function cannot be properly carried out without the willingness to be involved with confrontation. And, since confrontation usually involves personnel decisions, it is all the more difficult. Yet, confront we must if we are to be effective leaders. Fred Smith, a Christian businessman from Dallas, offers this insight:

> Whenever I am tempted not to act in a difficult personnel situation, I ask myself, "Am I holding back for my personal comfort or for the good of the organization?" If I am doing what makes me comfortable, I am embezzling. If doing what is good for the organization also happens to make me comfortable, that's wonderful. But if I am treating irresponsibility irresponsibly, I must remember that two wrongs do not make a right.[1]

Interestingly, the Bible has a lot to say about this subject and the leader is well advised to be alert to the biblical principles which ought to inform further thinking on this subject.

OPTIONS TO CONFRONTATION

David Augsburger, in his book *Caring Enough to Confront*,[2] states the various options to confrontation. First, the leader can choose to *ignore the problem*. This option is your basic "head-in-the-sand" approach. Perhaps the problem will go away if nothing is said or done. Surprisingly, many times this is the best option to consider. Leaders many times elevate insignificant incidents to the status of significant problems simply by agreeing to discuss the matter further. Since most leaders are not looking for additional work, this option to confrontation can be indeed useful. The insightful leader needs to be aware of *which* incidents ought to be handled this way and *when*.

The Old Testament story of Eli and his family is an illustration of the first option. God sent judgment to the house of Eli because of his wicked sons. Eli himself was judged "because of the sin he knew about; his sons made themselves contemptible, and he failed to restrain them" (1 Samuel 3:13). This was clearly a case where Eli ignored the problem.

A second option to confrontation is the *winner-take-all option*. In this situation, there is no such thing as compromise. There is always a winner and there is always a loser. No middle ground is allowed. I either win big or I lose big. America's frontier heritage characterized by the "shootout-at-OK-Corral" mentality has glamorized this approach to confrontation.

One example of this option from Scripture is the story of Absalom and David. As one of David's younger sons, Absalom probably realized that he would not be a likely candidate to succeed his father as king. So he set out on his "winner-take-all" game plan which included "stealing the hearts of the people," open sexual immorality with his father's wives, and open warfare against his father. Had he won by following this approach, the kingdom would have been his. He failed in his attempt, however— losing the war, his dignity, and his life.

Experience suggests that many in the Christian world use this option to deal with problems. It's characterized by an attitude that says, "Let's not discuss our concerns or deal with them forthrightly, but rather, let's start a new church, change churches or colleges, or move away." The landscape of the evangelical community is littered with the remains, both psychological and physical, of persons who chose this method of dealing with problems and who, having lost the battle, ultimately dropped out of the war.

A third option to confrontation is to *capitulate* or *give in to the concern*. This alternative assumes basically the opposite of the first option. I accede to the request and respond to the demands. I give them what they want.

A biblical example of this situation is found in 1 Kings 3. Two prostitutes, who shared the same house, came to Solomon with their tale of woe:

> Now two prostitutes came to the king and stood before him. One of them said, "My lord, this woman and I live in the same house. I had a baby while she was there with me. The third day after my child was born, this woman also had a baby. We were alone; there was no one in the house but the two of us.
>
> "During the night this woman's son died because she lay on him. So she got up in the middle of the night and took my son from my side while I your servant was asleep. She put him by her breast and put her dead son by my breast. The next morning, I got up to nurse my son—and he was dead! But when I looked at him closely in the morning light, I saw that it wasn't the son I had borne."
>
> The other woman said, "No! The living one is my son; the dead one is yours."
>
> But the first one insisted, "No! The dead one is yours; the living one is mine." And so they argued before the king.
>
> The king said, "This one says, 'My son is alive and your son is dead,' while that one says, 'No! Your son is dead and mine is alive.'"
>
> Then the king said, "Bring me a sword." So they brought a sword for the king. He then gave an order: "Cut the living child in two and give half to one and half to the other."
>
> The woman whose son was alive was filled with compassion for her son and said to the king, "Please, my lord, give her the living baby! Don't kill him!"

But the other said, "Neither I nor you shall have him. Cut him in two!"
Then the king gave his ruling: "Give the living baby to the first woman. Do not kill him; she is his mother" (1 Kings 3:16-27).

Solomon, in his God-given wisdom, knew that on some issues capitulating is not going nearly far enough. He knew that sometimes the person who has truth on his side will not settle for just half a loaf. This story, then, at once illustrates the dangers of acceding to a given request and the potential limitations of using this option to alleviate confrontation.

A fourth option to confrontation is the *"I'll-go-halfway-if-you'll-go-halfway"* approach. This option suggests that I have something worth hanging on to and I will work hard to hang on to my 50 percent. As long as I am able to hang on to part of my ideas or arguments, that is enough. I don't need to be the total winner. As a result, I don't need to be the total loser. Each side retains its dignity, so to speak. Each side is willing to compromise.

Probably one of the best biblical examples of using this approach for dealing with difficult issues is found in Acts 15, the story of the Jerusalem Council. A conflict had arisen about whether or not the new Gentile Christians had to submit to all of the Jewish traditions, such as circumcision, now that they had become believers. This issue was a highly emotional one and had the potential to splinter and fragment the early church, since many Jews were struggling with the concept of Gentiles being Christians in the first place.

Peter, who himself struggled with this issue, could have argued that the Jewish traditions were hopelessly out-of-date. Perhaps that position would have best satisfied Paul. Peter, however, didn't set forth that argument. Perhaps he knew that such a proposal would never have been agreed to by the Council. So instead, he suggested a compromise, one wherein the Jewish traditions would remain in place for Jews but the new Gentile believers would not be subject to them:

> Brothers, you know that some time ago God made a choice among you that the Gentiles might hear from my lips the message of the gospel and believe. God, who knows the

heart, showed that he accepted them by giving the Holy Spirit to them, just as he did to us. He made no distinction between us and them, for he purified their hearts by faith. Now then, why do you try to test God by putting on the necks of the disciples a yoke that neither we nor our fathers have been able to bear? (Acts 15:7-10)

Peter's proposal apparently was still too radical for the Jewish brethren, because what they ultimately agreed to was that Gentile Christians would still have a partial yoke, that is, they would have a much shorter list of Jewish traditions to adhere to:

Instead we should write to them, telling them to abstain from food polluted by idols, from sexual immorality, from the meat of strangled animals and from blood (Acts 15:20).

Even though it does not appear that Gentile Christians were present at this Council, those that ministered to them were. And it appears that this compromise solution was acceptable, for no dissent is recorded. In essence, what the Council agreed to was two different sets of church membership requirements, one for Jews and one for Gentiles. The singular success of this method for dealing with difficult issues suggests that it bears close consideration for use within our organizations.

While each of these options may sometime be used appropriately by the leader, there is a fifth option, and perhaps a better way—*the way of confrontation*—to deal with the difficult situations in leadership. As I use the term *confrontation*, I mean a willingness to look at an issue without a vested interest in the outcome, looking out always for the best interests of others. It may mean that my view won't be the prevailing one. It may mean that I'll "lose." But it also means that by involving myself in confrontation, I'm committing myself to a higher standard than simply winning or losing.

WHY CONFRONT?

A Christian leader has a twofold responsibility—not only to be effective in the leadership responsibility, but also to be faithful to the commands of Scripture. And one cannot read the pages of Scripture without being impressed that, as Christians, we are to be concerned, in a positive sense, about other believers. Note, for example, the following representative verses:

> Each of you should look not only to your own interests, but also to the interests of others (Philippians 2:4).

> Let the word of Christ dwell in you richly as you teach and admonish one another with all wisdom, and as you sing psalms, hymns and spiritual songs with gratitude in your hearts to God (Colossians 3:16).

> And let us consider how we may spur one another on toward love and good deeds. Let us not give up meeting together, as some are in the habit of doing, but let us encourage one another—and all the more as you see the Day approaching (Hebrews 10:24-25).

> Carry each other's burdens, and in this way you will fulfill the law of Christ (Galatians 6:2).

As Christians, we confront not to embarrass, belittle, tear down, or humiliate. We confront because of our commitment to help others reach their potential, including full-fledged stature in Christ. Paul had to say some very difficult things to the readers of his letters, but it was because of his unwavering bottom-line commitment to people:

> And we pray this in order that you may live a life worthy of the Lord and may please him in every way: bearing fruit in every good work, growing in the knowledge of God (Colossians 1:10).

In education, one of the distinctions frequently made regarding evaluation is the difference between *formative* evaluation and *summative* evaluation. Formative evaluation is the process of giving ongoing feedback to an individual, thus enabling him to make appropriate midstream corrections and do a better job. "John, we need to place more emphasis on that item rather than this one." "Mary, let's use more written work rather than solely oral reports." Summative evaluation has more of a sense of finality to it. "John, as of May 1, you will no longer have a job here." "Mary, your contract will not be renewed after it expires this year." I use the concept of confrontation, at least in terms of our initial focus, to be somewhat analogous to this concept of formative evaluation. Certainly, summative activity will at times be necessary but rarely should it be the first-strike response of the Christian leader.

My experience with Christian organizations is that very little formative evaluation is done and an overemphasis is placed on summative evaluation. It's not unusual for an individual to be fired and not have any idea why. When reasons *are* given, they usually have not been preceded by the employer's earlier concerns. Thus the individual goes without opportunity for correction and the organization's commitment to help him improve.

With these preliminary thoughts out of the way, let's now look at some biblical perspectives on this difficult subject.

PERSPECTIVES ON CONFRONTATION

Without question, *confrontation is hard.* I have yet to meet the Christian leader who relished the opportunity to confront difficult situations or difficult people. Indeed, the person who enjoys firing people needs to be alert to checking the motivation level—the wrong kind of motivation may be a problem. Since termination usually has a variety of negative ramifications for the organization and for the leader (e.g., morale, economic, psychological, legal), if someone tells me that firing people is one of the more enjoyable parts of the job, I become worried, not only for the individual but also for the organization which that leader directs.

Paul, on several occasions, discusses the difficulty of confronting people. Notice, for example, this passage:

> I call upon this God to witness against me if I am not telling the absolute truth: the reason I haven't come to visit you yet is that I don't want to sadden you with a severe rebuke. When I come, although I can't do much to help your faith, for it is strong already, I want to be able to do something about your joy: I want to make you happy, not sad.
>
> "No," I said to myself, "I won't do it. I'll not make them unhappy with another painful visit." For if I make you sad, who is going to make me happy? You are the ones to do it, and how can you if I cause you pain? That is why I wrote as I did in my last letter, so that you will get things straightened

out before I come. Then, when I do come, I will not be made sad by the very ones who ought to give me greatest joy. I felt sure that your happiness was so bound up in mine that you would not be happy either, unless I came with joy.

Oh, how I hated to write that letter! It almost broke my heart and I tell you honestly that I cried over it. I didn't want to hurt you, but I had to show you how very much I loved you and cared about what was happening to you (2 Corinthians 1:23–2:4, TLB).

Make no mistake—for Paul and for many leaders confrontation of people is painfully difficult.

Secondly, leaders must *create an environment wherein both leader and followers are prepared—indeed, expect—to be confronted.* Note the Scripture on this principle (all verses quoted from *The Living Bible*):

Anyone willing to be corrected is on the pathway to life. Anyone refusing has lost his chance (Proverbs 10:17).

To learn, you must want to be taught. To refuse reproof is stupid (Proverbs 12:1).

A fool thinks he needs no advice, but a wise man listens to others (Proverbs 12:15).

Punish a mocker and others will learn from his example. Reprove a wise man and he will be the wiser (Proverbs 19:25).

Don't refuse to accept criticism; get all the help you can (Proverbs 23:12).

It is a badge of honor to accept valid criticism (Proverbs 25:12).

A man who refuses to admit his mistakes can never be successful. But if he confesses and forsakes them, he gets another chance (Proverbs 28:13).

In the end, people appreciate frankness more than flattery (Proverbs 28:23).

Contrary to what might be expected, the sense of these

verses suggests that people not only ought to be ready for confrontation but that they should be eager to receive it. The idea seems to be, "I'll be less than effective as a leader if I fail to develop an institutional climate where persons feel free to confront me." One of my staff members has even noted with regard to confrontation that it's more blessed to receive than to give. In short, by establishing a climate conducive to healthy confrontation, both individuals and the organization have the potential for positive growth.

Of course, people will not always respond to confrontation the way we would like, as Scripture plainly indicates:

> We all have happy memories of good men gone to their reward, but the names of wicked men stink after them. The wise man is glad to be instructed, but a self-sufficient fool falls flat on his face. A good man has firm footing, but a crook will slip and fall (Proverbs 10:7-9, TLB).

> Whoever loves discipline loves knowledge, but he who hates correction is stupid (Proverbs 12:1).

Further, Paul records the reactions of the Corinthians to some of his more difficult, confrontive letters:

> Even if I caused you sorrow by my letter, I do not regret it. Though I did regret it—I see that my letter hurt you, but only for a little while—yet now I am happy, not because you were made sorry, but because your sorrow led you to repentance. For you became sorrowful as God intended and so were not harmed in any way by us. Godly sorrow brings repentance that leads to salvation and leaves no regret, but worldly sorrow brings death. See what this godly sorrow has produced in you: what earnestness, what eagerness to clear yourselves, what indignation, what alarm, what longing, what concern, what readiness to see justice done. At every point you have proved yourselves to be innocent in this matter (2 Corinthians 7:8-11).

These verses and others suggest that we ought to be "on notice" that people who care about us and the organization we lead will be confronting us. When that happens, we should look for the good in it and learn from it—even though sometimes the confrontation may not be totally on target. Many persons react defensively to confrontation, even to the point of saying, "How dare you challenge my thinking or decision." The Proverbs suggest that this response is not in keeping with other biblical principles.

When King David was in the midst of escaping his rebellious son Absalom, a man named Shimei started to do something that every leader has experienced—he called David names, threw stones, and told him it was time to quit: "Get out, get out, you man of blood, you scoundrel!" (2 Samuel 16:7) David's defenders asked permission to take the life of this oppressor of God's chosen leader. David refused, however, and his response reflects the kind of openness that leaders ought to have regarding confrontation and/or criticism:

> Then Abishai son of Zeruiah said to the king, "Why should this dead dog curse my lord the king? Let me go over and cut off his head."
> But the king said, "What do you and I have in common, you sons of Zeruiah? If he is cursing because the Lord said to him, 'Curse David,' who can ask, 'Why do you do this?' "
> David then said to Abishai and all his officials, "My son, who is of my own flesh, is trying to take my life. How much more, then, this Benjamite! Leave him alone; let him curse, for the Lord has told him to. It may be that the Lord will see my distress and repay me with good for the cursing I am receiving today" (2 Samuel 16:9-12).

Later on, when David had reclaimed the throne and Absalom was dead, David's staff reminded him that since Shimei's curses were obviously unjust, David should now give him his due. David, however, did not see it that way:

> They crossed at the ford to take the king's household over and to do whatever he wished. When Shimei son of Gera crossed the Jordan, he fell prostrate before the king and said to him, "May my lord not hold me guilty. Do not remember how your servant did wrong on the day my lord the king left Jerusalem. May the king put it out of his mind. For I your

servant know that I have sinned, but today I have come here as the first of the whole house of Joseph to come down and meet my lord the king."

Then Abishai son of Zeruiah said, "Shouldn't Shimei be put to death for this? He cursed the Lord's anointed."

David replied, "What do you and I have in common, you sons of Zeruiah? This day you have become my adversaries! Should anyone be put to death in Israel today? Do I not know that today I am king over Israel?" So the king said to Shimei, "You shall not die." And the king promised him on oath (2 Samuel 19:18-23).

David's forbearance illustrates not only his openness to confrontation (also illustrated by his response to the Prophet Nathan in 2 Samuel 12), but also his forgiving spirit.

Thirdly, Scripture also suggests that *leaders need to be continually involved in self-confrontation*, using God's Word as their standard. I don't believe Scripture teaches that I can ignore everything in my own life and be concerned only about what others do or how they perform. Jesus in fact had some harsh words for the Pharisees because they seemed more concerned about the specks in others' eyes than the beams in their own:

Why do you look at the speck of sawdust in your brother's eye and pay no attention to the plank in your own eye? How can you say to your brother, "Brother, let me take the speck out of your eye," when you yourself fail to see the plank in your own eye? You hypocrite, first take the plank out of your eye, and then you will see clearly to remove the speck from your brother's eye (Luke 6:41-42).

This self-confrontation ought not to be viewed as a debasing experience but rather as a way I deal with my limitations as a leader so that I can be all that God wants me to be for His glory. Our approach must reflect that discussed by James when he wrote we are not only to be hearers of the Word but also doers of it:

Do not merely listen to the word, and so deceive yourselves. Do what it says. Anyone who listens to the word but does not do what it says is like a man who looks at his face in a mirror and, after looking at himself, goes away and immediately forgets what he looks like. But the man who looks intently into the perfect law that gives freedom, and continues to do this, not forgetting what he has heard, but doing it—he will be blessed in what he does (James 1:22-25).

Fourthly, *confrontation of others must be done with great humility and respect for personhood.* The leader's attitude during confrontation must reflect the kind of sensitivity to others illustrated in these New Testament exhortations:

Be devoted to one another in brotherly love. Honor one another above yourselves (Romans 12:10).

And the Lord's servant must not quarrel; instead, he must be kind to everyone, able to teach, not resentful (2 Timothy 2:24).

By the meekness and gentleness of Christ, I appeal to you— I, Paul, who am "timid" when face to face with you, but "bold" when away! (2 Corinthians 10:1)

Brothers, if someone is caught in a sin, you who are spiritual should restore him gently. But watch yourselves, or you also may be tempted (Galatians 6:1).

Leaders must be neither overeager nor too hesitant to confront. Again, I confront not because it makes me feel good but because I, as a leader, am committed to both the organization's goals *and* to seeing a brother or sister mature in Christ.

BIBLICAL EXAMPLES

The entire Book of Philemon is an excellent case study on confrontation. Philemon was a slave owner who had a runaway slave, Onesimus. Apparently this runaway slave had come under the influence of Paul's teaching ministry and had given his heart to Christ. Probably in some splendid one-on-one sessions, Onesimus had explained his difficult situation to Paul, who also happened to know Philemon. How was this difficult situation to be resolved? Paul decided to confront Philemon directly about the matter, and the result is the magnificent letter preserved for eternity in the

New Testament. But just how did Paul confront Philemon?

First, *Paul started on a positive note.* The words he chose, words such as *dear friend* and *grace and peace to you* are positive words.

Second, *he affirmed in Philemon positive character qualities*:

> I always thank my God as I remember you in my prayers, because I hear about your faith in the Lord Jesus and your love for all the saints. I pray that you may be active in sharing your faith, so that you will have a full understanding of every good thing we have in Christ. Your love has given me great joy and encouragement, because you, brother, have refreshed the hearts of the saints (vv. 4-7).

Third, *Paul based his approach in love and gentleness.* Paul observed that even though he could demand that Philemon respond in a particular way, he wanted to appeal to him on the basis of love (v. 9).

Fourth, *Paul made his request* (vv. 9-15). Effective confrontation must deal with specifics and particulars. Generalities and otherwise vague statements might be less painful for the one doing the confronting, but they will be ineffective. The one being confronted must understand fully what is the concern.

Fifth, *Paul was willing to be personally responsible to help right the wrong*: "If he has done you any wrong or owes you anything, charge it to me" (v. 18). An effective confronter must not only be specific in the concern, but must also commit himself/herself to help rectify the concern.

Finally, *Paul anticipated a positive response to his confrontation of Philemon*: "Confident of your obedience, I write to you, knowing that you will do even more than I ask" (v. 21). The text doesn't tell us how Philemon actually responded to the confrontation, but there seems to be little doubt that, confronted this way, Philemon would choose to treat Onesimus far better than runaway slaves were normally treated. Very few of us would object to being confronted the way Paul went about confronting Philemon. Leaders would learn much from following this marvelous case study.

A second biblical example of positive confrontation is found in Joshua 22. Joshua was overseeing the leadership function of ensuring that each of the tribes of Israel received its proper inheritance. He had just told the Reubenites, the Gadites, and the half-tribe of Manasseh that they could return to their land back across the Jordan River in keeping with an earlier decision of Moses. Joshua also reminded them of their continuing obligation to follow the Lord "in all his ways" (Joshua 22:5).

As soon as these tribes returned to their homes, they built an imposing altar which offended the remaining ten tribes, who prepared "to go to war against them" (v. 12). Before the war began, however, the Israelites sent a fact-finding group across the Jordan to confront the "offenders" about their decision to "break faith with the God of Israel" (v. 16). There they learned that the "offending" parties had no intention of breaking God's law and instead, had built the monument as a reminder to all of their key part in the nation of Israel. When this good report was brought back, the people "were glad to hear the report and praised God. And they talked no more about going to war against them" (v. 33). Here, confrontation resulted in clarification which ultimately saved much unnecessary bloodshed and organizational heartache.

In conclusion, confrontation is one of the least glamorous and most difficult facets of leadership. It is, however, one of leadership's most necessary and important responsibilities. Failure to confront produces negative results for both persons and the organization. Only as the art of confrontation is carried out under the divine leadership of the Holy Spirit will the kind of personal and organizational results desired by leaders be accomplished.

FORGIVENESS

A leader who has not learned to be a good forgiver will not be as effective a leader as one who has. Leadership affords too many uncomfortable incidents, too many inaccurate accusations, and too little time to keep track of everyone who has "wronged" you.

To place the subject of forgiveness in some kind of a context, pretend for a moment that next week the local high-school auditorium will feature a dramatic presentation of your life story. The story will feature everything you've ever done. Everything! Nothing will be left out. In addition, the story will feature everything you've ever said. Everything! To make it even more spectacular, it will feature everything you've ever thought. Everything! Not very many leaders I know, including me, would want to come forward after a presentation like that to take a bow. Most of us would probably beat a path to the door as quickly as possible and vanish from sight.

Some leaders are probably thinking, "I'm sure glad nobody has a recorded story like that of my life." The truth of the matter, however, is that somebody *does* have that story—unless we've experienced the forgiveness of Christ in our lives. The psalmist states that "as far as the east is from the west, so far has he removed our transgressions from us" (Psalm 103:12).

At the heart of the Gospel of Jesus Christ is forgiveness. Christ died for sins even while we were yet sinners. Because He paid the penalty for sin, I have experienced His forgiveness. And each time that I sin, I continue to seek His forgiveness. I'm told that "he who conceals his sins does not prosper, but whoever confesses and renounces them finds mercy" (Proverbs 28:13). And in the New Testament: "If we confess our sins, he is faithful and just and will forgive us our sins and purify us from all unrighteousness" (1 John 1:9). Simply put, as a forgiven person, and as a leader, I must be a forgiving person.

The idea that comes to us from the pages of Scripture features a two-dimensional concept of forgiveness. First, and as already has been noted, we need to experience forgiveness at the vertical dimension—between ourselves and God. Second, God wants us to experience forgiveness at the horizontal level— person to person. As we'll see, failure to forgive persons at the horizontal level produces a devastating impact on our relationship with God on the vertical level.

This chapter will deal with the following questions: Why forgive? Who is responsible to initiate forgiveness? How many times must I forgive? What are the consequences if I don't forgive? What does forgiveness involve?

WHY FORGIVE?

One of the fundamental arguments for horizontal forgiveness is that we are to forgive one another because Christ is our example. Note Paul's instructions:

> Bear with each other and forgive whatever grievances you may have against one another. Forgive as the Lord forgave you (Colossians 3:13).

> Be kind and compassionate to one another, forgiving each other, just as in Christ God forgave you (Ephesians 4:32).

What Paul clearly commands is this: you have been forgiven by Christ, so you should forgive others. Simply put, a leader does not have the option not to forgive others. We are to forgive because Scripture commands it.

WHO INITIATES FORGIVENESS?

Without question, *the person responsible for causing the offense in the first place has a responsibility to initiate the forgiveness process.* In other words, if I, as the leader, have done something to offend someone, I have a responsibility to go to that person and ask forgiveness. This assumes, of course, that I know that I have been the source of offense.

Jesus talked about this type of situation in the Sermon on the Mount:

> Therefore, if you are offering your gift at the altar and there remember that your brother has something against you, leave your gift there in front of the altar. First go and be reconciled to your brother; then come and offer your gift (Matthew 5:23-24).

The idea is this. I'm standing in front of the altar getting ready to offer my sacrifice when I remember that my brother has something against me—presumably because of something I've done to him. What am I to do? As important as sacrifice and religious ceremony are, Jesus says that it is even more important to be reconciled to my brother. Therefore, I am to leave my gift or sacrifice at the altar, go seek my brother's forgiveness, and return to finish offering my sacrifice.

With regard to forgiveness, time is of the essence. We need to keep short accounts. So if we have to choose between going to church on Sunday morning or going to seek reconciliation with a brother, we are to first seek reconciliation. Notice, however, that Jesus doesn't provide an either/or choice. He doesn't say, "Choose religious ceremony or pursue forgiveness." Rather, He seems to be suggesting that horizontal forgiveness ought to come before religious ceremony, and further that our willingness to participate in the forgiveness process will affect our ability to worship.

I want to emphasize that this text appears to apply only to those situations where you remember "that your brother has something against you." Many times people are offended by something the leader has done, but the leader has no idea that his or her actions have been offensive. In my experience as a leader people rarely tell me directly that I have offended them. Rather, I find out second- or thirdhand. This lack of directness is unfortunate, but once I know that I have been the source of the offense, the responsibility is still mine to initiate forgiveness.

Having said that, I also believe that Scripture teaches that *the one offended has a responsibility to initiate the forgiveness process.* Two texts which illustrate this principle are Mark 11:25 and Luke 17:1-10. In the Mark text, Jesus taught: "And when you stand praying, if you hold anything against anyone, forgive him, so that your Father in heaven may forgive you your sins." Whereas the Matthew 5 text was addressed to those who knew someone was upset because of something they did, this text is addressed to those who are upset because they have been offended by another, whether or not the offender is aware of it. Unlike the Matthew text, where the one at the altar had the responsibility to immediately go to the other brother to make it right, this text simply suggests that if I am offended by something you've done, whether or not you know I'm upset about it, I have the responsibility to forgive you. If my forgiving you is primarily attitudinal, perhaps I don't even need to tell you about it. The point is, the one offended does not have the option to wait until the alleged offender initiates forgiveness. He (or she) has his own affirmative burden or obligation to make things right.

If any doubt existed about what Jesus intended to say about the responsibility regarding the one offended, He made the point quite clear when He said to His disciples:

> So watch yourselves. If your brother sins, rebuke him, and if he repents, forgive him. If he sins against you seven times in a day, and seven times comes back to you and says, "I repent," forgive him (Luke 17:3-4).

No wonder that the disciples' response to this "impossible" teaching was, "Increase our faith" (v. 5). Yet in the verses that immediately follow, Jesus emphasized that forgiveness doesn't require more faith as much as it requires simple obedience:

> Suppose one of you had a servant plowing or looking after the sheep. Would he say to the servant when he comes in from the field, "Come along now and sit down to eat"? Would he not rather say, "Prepare my supper, get yourself ready and wait on me while I eat and drink; after that you may eat and drink"? Would he thank the servant because he did what he was told to do? So you also, when you have done everything you were told to do, should say, "We are

unworthy servants; we have only done our duty" (Luke 17:7-10).

Here, then, is an affirmative responsibility and an implied duty for the one offended to heal the wounds. Interestingly, Jesus places the burden for initiating forgiveness on both the person committing the offense as well as on the one offended. Not surprisingly, He covers all the bases.

For those in leadership positions, this comes as good news. Most leaders represent a broad and diverse group of constituencies. In a Christian college, for example, some of the competing groups include trustees, the students, faculty, parents, alumni, a supporting church, the community, and donors. Obviously, leaders have the responsibility to make sure their actions are not unnecessarily offensive (rarely do leaders do something not offensive to somebody!). Where leaders know they have offended someone, they need to pursue and request forgiveness. But the burden is not all on leaders. People whom leaders may have unknowingly offended have the responsibility to approach the leaders to make things right as well.

DOES THE LEADER HAVE TO FORGIVE?

Does the leader have the option not to extend forgiveness to a brother or sister who requests it? The biblical record seems to answer that question with an unequivocal no. In other words, if a person repents and seeks forgiveness in the name of Christ, forgiveness must be extended.

Mark 11:25 goes so far as to say that if a person fails to extend forgiveness to another, then the Father in heaven will not extend forgiveness to the one refusing to forgive. In essence, Jesus says, "If you want My Father's forgiveness, then extend forgiveness to others."

Perhaps one of Jesus' strongest statements on the obligation to extend forgiveness is found in the parable recorded in Matthew 18:23-35:

> The kingdom of heaven is like a king who wanted to settle accounts with his servants. As he began the settlement, a man who owed him ten thousand talents was brought to him. Since he was not able to pay, the master ordered that

he and his wife and his children and all that he had be sold to repay the debt.

The servant fell on his knees before him. "Be patient with me," he begged, "and I will pay back everything." The servant's master took pity on him, canceled the debt and let him go.

But when that servant went out, he found one of his fellow servants who owed him a hundred denarii. He grabbed him and began to choke him. "Pay back what you owe me!" he demanded.

His fellow servant fell to his knees and begged him, "Be patient with me, and I will pay you back."

But he refused. Instead, he went off and had the man thrown into prison until he could pay the debt. When the other servants saw what had happened, they were greatly distressed and went and told their master everything that had happened.

Then the master called the servant in. "You wicked servant," he said, "I canceled all that debt of yours because you begged me to. Shouldn't you have had mercy on your fellow servant just as I had on you?" In anger his master turned him over to the jailers until he should pay back all he owed.

This is how my heavenly Father will treat each of you unless you forgive your brother from your heart.

When the master who had forgiven much heard how the unmerciful servant was unwilling to forgive little, he in essence took back his forgiveness (that is, he reinstated the large debt in its entirety!) and threw the unmerciful servant into prison. Applying this story to his listeners, Jesus warned them that "this is how my heavenly Father will treat each of you unless you forgive your brother from your heart." Further, He pointed out the dire consequences that await the person who refuses to forgive.

HOW MUCH MUST A LEADER FORGIVE?
Jesus apparently anticipated this kind of question because He addressed it on several occasions. In the Luke 17 passage, He observed that if a person sins against another seven times in one day and yet repents seven times, forgiveness must be extended.

Peter was probably counting the number of times he had forgiven someone because according to Matthew 18:21-22 he wanted to clarify the issue with Jesus: "Then Peter came to Jesus and asked, 'Lord, how many times shall I forgive my brother when he sins against me? Up to seven times?' " Jesus in essence told Peter to quit counting and learn once and for all that extending forgiveness to others needs to be viewed as a way of life for the Christian, no matter how many times he has been wronged: "Jesus answered, 'I tell you, not seven times, but seventy-seven times' " (v. 22).

WHAT ABOUT "BAD" SINS?

Does the leader (and others, for that matter) have to be forgiven "bad" sins? The obvious inference here is that there are "good" sins, which are not worthy of significant organizational response and which can be forgiven. And then there are "bad" sins, which, if committed by the leader or others, and even when forgiveness is extended, will almost surely result in dismissal.

These kinds of issues are seldom discussed in Christian publications. Sins relating to sexuality (particularly affairs and divorce) and criminal conduct figure prominently as "bad" sins. Leaders and others who commit them, even when all parties extend and are extended forgiveness, can count on job-hunting. Why?

Perhaps the matter would not be so troubling if the reason for the decision to dismiss were tied to matters such as "holiness of life" and organizational purity. Many times, however, the reason for the dismissal is based primarily on the rationale that continued employment "will be bad for our ministry. After all, people won't support our ministry if a forgiven adulterer serves as our leader. Monetary gifts would stop and, obviously, the organization needs money to operate." And the organization definitely doesn't want its supporters to think it is "soft on sin." "Look how God punished Achan" (see biblical references such as Joshua 7), proponents of this view say. But what about David and the abominable sins he committed—lust, adultery, and murder? Did God remove him from office? The answer, obviously, is no. Of course, even though David confessed his sin and was forgiven by God, there were still consequences for his sin. Nathan the prophet announced God's judgment:

Now, therefore, the sword will never depart from your house, because you despised me and took the wife of Uriah the Hittite to be your own.

This is what the Lord says: "Out of your own household I am going to bring calamity upon you. Before your very eyes I will take your wives and give them to one who is close to you, and he will lie with your wives in broad daylight. You did it in secret, but I will do this thing in broad daylight before all Israel."

Then David said to Nathan, "I have sinned against the Lord."

Nathan replied, "The Lord has taken away your sin. You are not going to die. But because by doing this you have made the enemies of the Lord show utter contempt, the son born to you will die" (2 Samuel 12:10-14).

Because of David's sin, his son died and internal warfare within the royal family resulted. However, David was not removed from his position of leadership. Again, the question is raised—why not?

Perhaps the contemporary Christian organization has made one of its highest priorities keeping its constituency happy and the religious influencers satisfied rather than having Christ be its guide and example. Did not Jesus have His harshest criticism for the religious community? If David were a contemporary leader in a leading evangelical organization and, assuming he genuinely confessed his sin, would there be doubt in anyone's mind that he would be removed from his position of leadership? Why would God not remove David and why would we? Perhaps it's because we yet fail to understand how God works within His people and what forgiveness really involves.

Another example of forgiveness involves Peter. This man was one of the Lord's closest friends and disciples for several years. In organizational parlance, he would have been considered a senior-level executive. At a point of pressure, however, he totally denied any knowledge of the group he worked with, especially its leader. Again, had this taken place in the contemporary Christian organization, Peter would no doubt be on the street—fired from his job. But what did Jesus do? He not only forgave Peter, but He made him into an important pillar of the early church. Why was Jesus so "radical" on this matter of forgiveness?

Perhaps we get additional insight on this issue by reviewing the events set forth in Luke 7:36-50. Here, a sinful woman came unannounced to a dinner in honor of Jesus hosted by Simon, a local religious leader. The woman brought expensive perfume, and falling at Jesus' feet, used her hair and tears from her weeping to wipe Jesus' feet before pouring the perfume on them. Simon immediately challenged Christ's deity because, he concluded in his mind, if He really were a prophet, He would have known about this woman and would not have had anything to do with her.

Jesus read Simon's mind and then proceeded to tell him a story about two men, each of whom owed a "moneylender" money. One of the debtors owed the moneylender an amount ten times larger than the other, but because neither had the money to repay him, the moneylender canceled both men's debts. Jesus then asked Simon a key question: "Now which of them will love him more?" (Luke 7:42)

The man replied, "I suppose the one who had the bigger debt canceled" (v. 43).

Jesus affirmed the correctness of Simon's answer, then added, "Therefore, I tell you, her many sins have been forgiven—for she loved much. But he who has been forgiven little loves little" (v. 47). Jesus in essence said that the "bad"-yet-forgiven sinner will love Him best because that person realizes the magnitude of what has been forgiven.

A similar situation is presented in the Parable of the Prodigal (or Lost) Son in Luke 15, a story we'll deal with in greater depth later in this chapter. The "other" brother, much like Simon in the previous parable, could not understand how his father could forgive his "bad" brother and restore him to his place in the family, especially since he had always been "good" and never merited such special attention. In fact, the "other" brother refused to participate in the celebration of reconciliation. Jesus must have really made the Pharisees angry when He observed that the kingdom of God operates by this very principle of forgiveness, even for the most sin-stained of persons.

These and other scriptural situations—where both horizontal and vertical forgiveness and confession are genuine—suggest, at least in the organizational context, that forgiven persons will ultimately be even better employees than they were before their sinning ways because they have been forgiven much. If such individuals were retained by the organization, whether restored to their previous leadership positions or not, perhaps they might be even more effective and committed employees.

Certainly, this discussion is not intended in any way to encourage the pursuit of one's sinful ways because "after all, I'll be forgiven and I won't lose my job." When the Apostle Paul was discussing the relationship among God's grace, law, and sin, he addressed the issue this way: "What shall we say then? Shall we go on sinning so that grace may increase? By no means! We died to sin; how can we live in it any longer?" (Romans 6:1-2)

The leader "dead to sin" clearly is not the one who in a calculating kind of way does an analysis of the costs and benefits of some anticipated future sin. Paul's instruction on this point is clear:

> In the same way, count yourselves dead to sin but alive to God in Christ Jesus. Therefore do not let sin reign in your mortal body so that you obey its evil desires. Do not offer the parts of your body to sin, as instruments of wickedness, but rather offer yourselves to God, as those who have been brought from death to life; and offer the parts of your body to him as instruments of righteousness. For sin shall not be your master, because you are not under law, but under grace (Romans 6:11-14).

Sadly, many Christians today have not only gone soft on sin, but are no longer able to identify what sin really is. Indeed, many persons have rarely, if ever, heard a sermon defining sin. Everyone, however, presumably knows what sin is, and unspokenly categorizes it into two groups: (1) *socially acceptable sins* such as pride, greed, gossiping, slander, and divisiveness—all of which usually result in little if any organizational sanction, and (2) *socially unacceptable sins*, such as alcohol abuse, drug use, sexual immorality—which almost always lead to dismissal from the organization. Within each group, each sin is ranked according to its degree of sinfulness.

Further, we have transformed our sin list into a much shorter organizational list of "do's and don'ts," though many items on it are more "cultural" concerns than biblical absolutes. If people "do the do's" and "don't the don'ts," they end up feeling pretty good about themselves. Unfortunately for these people, the Bible doesn't differentiate between socially acceptable and socially unacceptable sins. Disobedience in God's eyes is sin, no matter if we try to relegate some of it to lesser status.

The Book of Proverbs, for example, includes a variety of wrongs on its sin list:

> There are six things the Lord hates, seven that are detestable to him: haughty eyes, a lying tongue, hands that shed innocent blood, a heart that devises wicked schemes, feet that are quick to rush into evil, a false witness who pours out lies and a man who stirs up dissension among brothers (Proverbs 6:16-19).

James 4:17 suggests that if we know how to do good and don't do it, our inaction is sin. First John makes it clear that if we fail to follow or obey the commands of Jesus, we are liars:

> We know that we have come to know him if we obey his commands. The man who says, "I know him," but does not do what he commands is a liar, and the truth is not in him. But if anyone obeys his word, God's love is truly made complete in him. This is how we know we are in him: Whoever claims to live in him must walk as Jesus did (1 John 2:3-6).

Jesus said the same thing in John 14:15 and 15:14, respectively: "If you love me, you will obey what I command." "You are my friends if you do what I command." In other words, "You know My commands. Keep them. Those of you who do, love Me. Those of you who don't are living in sin." This emphasis on measuring our love for Him by what we do rather than what we say is made crystal clear in another passage:

> When the Son of Man comes in his glory, and all the angels with him, he will sit on his throne in heavenly glory. All the nations will be gathered before him, and he will separate the people one from another as a shepherd separates the sheep from the goats. He will put the sheep on his right and the goats on his left.

Then the King will say to those on his right, "Come, you who are blessed by my Father; take your inheritance, the kingdom prepared for you since the creation of the world. For I was hungry and you gave me something to eat, I was thirsty and you gave me something to drink, I was a stranger and you invited me in, I needed clothes and you clothed me, I was sick and you looked after me, I was in prison and you came to visit me."

Then the righteous will answer him, "Lord, when did we see you hungry and feed you, or thirsty and give you something to drink? When did we see you a stranger and invite you in, or needing clothes and clothe you? When did we see you sick or in prison and go to visit you?"

The King will reply, "I tell you the truth, whatever you did for one of the least of these brothers of mine, you did for me."

Then he will say to those on his left, "Depart from me, you who are cursed, into the eternal fire prepared for the devil and his angels. For I was hungry and you gave me nothing to eat, I was thirsty and you gave me nothing to drink, I was a stranger and you did not invite me in, I needed clothes and you did not clothe me, I was sick and in prison and you did not look after me."

They also will answer, "Lord, when did we see you hungry or thirsty or a stranger or needing clothes or sick or in prison, and did not help you?"

He will reply, "I tell you the truth, whatever you did not do for one of the least of these, you did not do for me."

Then they will go away to eternal punishment, but the righteous to eternal life (Matthew 25:31-46).

In this passage, the primary difference between and subsequent judgment of the two groups was based on what one group didn't do and what the other group did do.

WHAT IF FORGIVENESS IS NOT EXTENDED?

Earlier discussion of the Parable of the Unmerciful Servant (Matthew 18:23-25) suggested that failure to forgive produced dire consequences. Mark 11:25 specifically suggested that failure to forgive results in the Heavenly Father's failure to forgive the sin of the one withholding forgiveness. To make the point again, after His instruction on how to pray, Jesus added these words of caution: "For if you forgive men when they sin against you, your heavenly Father will also forgive you. But if you do not forgive men their sins, your Father will not forgive your sins" (Matthew 6:14-15).

Given these dire consequences regarding the failure to forgive, it is shocking and surprising to witness the number of grudges, infightings, and political battles that many times plague Christian organizations. Perhaps one of the most important responsibilities of leaders is not only to make sure that accounts are kept short between them and others, but also to endeavor to ensure that forgiveness is practiced throughout the organization. Given the biblical emphasis on unity, and Jesus' statement that the world would know His disciples by the love they had one for another, it is not extraordinary that His teaching on the subject of forgiveness is so powerful and that the consequences of failing to follow this instruction so extreme.

WHAT IF I DON'T FEEL LIKE FORGIVING?

If something is done without feeling, does that make the action ungenuine? No, I think not. Frequently the leader is called to do things that he or she may not feel like doing. The same is true in my personal life. For example, I don't feel like getting up early every morning, yet I do. Does that make me a hypocrite? Surely not. What would make me a hypocrite is going around telling everyone how much I enjoy getting up early in the morning. Some of Jesus' harshest words were targeted toward the Pharisees who constantly were trying to project an outward image to the people that didn't match their heart attitude.

In the context of forgiveness, if someone has offended me, it is not necessary that I feel like forgiving him in order to extend forgiveness. That is not hypocrisy. What would make the act hypocritical would be for me to state how much I've enjoyed extending forgiveness when in fact I've hated doing so. Time and time again, the leader is called to go against feelings to be a responsible leader and a responsible Christian. And when dealing with the issue of forgiveness, many times the leader may have to go against feelings. In the Luke 17 passage examined earlier, Jesus seems to be saying, "Don't even consider the fact that I ask you to forgive and forgive and forgive to be a big deal. Rather, consider your response to be analagous to the hired hand who is simply doing his duty."

WHAT DOES FORGIVENESS INVOLVE?

According to a noted counselor, forgiveness involves at least three facets. First, when I forgive, in essence I say that *I will not raise the matter again.* Our example, again, is the person of Christ and His relationship to me. When He forgives me, He obliterates the record.

Second, extending forgiveness means that after forgiveness has been extended, *I will not tell other persons about the previously committed wrong.* The matter of offense becomes a closed one between the two parties.

Third, after forgiveness has been extended, *I will not dwell on the matter myself.* The person who says, "I'll forgive you but I'll never forget it" has not really extended forgiveness. Granted, I may have to work at forgetting, but work at it I must. In the Parable of the Unmerciful Servant, Jesus addressed this issue in part by stating that forgiveness had to eventually affect the heart: "Unless you *forgive* your brother *from your heart*" (Matthew 18:35, italics added).

It is tempting to conclude from this discussion that if forgiveness is so important, then as long as a leader, or any employee for that matter, who fails requests forgiveness—whether from the board, the people, or from others—there need be no accountability or consequences.

Further, if forgiveness involves the three facets just mentioned, are such criteria applicable in an organizational context? For instance, what if an employee fails miserably and repeatedly in the performance of an assigned task, but asks and is granted forgiveness? Is the leader violating a biblical principle if such failures are later noted in personnel files and thereafter used to support a subsequent decision to terminate employment? Is the concept of forgiveness limited to the personal, theological dimensions of life and not to the organizational ones?

In reply, nowhere does Scripture suggest that forgiveness and accountability are mutually exclusive concepts. For example, Moses' failure to properly follow God's instructions ultimately deprived him of the opportunity not only to lead but also to enter the Promised Land. God forgave the Israelites for their disobedience of unbelief (Numbers 14:20), but they still had to wander in the desert for forty years. As mentioned earlier, David's sin with Bathsheba was forgiven, but nonetheless produced dire consequences for his family. On the other hand, the biblical texts clearly state the leader's obligation to extend forgiveness when such is requested, that the leader needs to be prepared to extend forgiveness an unlimited number of times, and that forgiveness must be practiced both on and off of the job. In any case, organizational application of the matter of forgiveness is indeed a difficult issue.

CASE STUDIES

Two case studies on forgiveness from Scripture—one from the Old Testament and one from the New—conclude this chapter. Both deal with leaders, one a powerful politician and the other a dynamic businessman. Both also deal with family problems.

The first is the account of Joseph recorded in Genesis 37–50. Because of his dreams which often depicted him in a superior position to his siblings, Joseph's older brothers hated him. At last they sold him into slavery in Egypt, where after a series of "misfortunate" events, the Pharaoh made Joseph prime minister.

Years later, a famine forced Joseph's brothers to go to Egypt for grain, a commodity now controlled by Joseph. When Joseph saw his brothers, he was not immediately prepared to offer them forgiveness. Indeed, he pretended to be a stranger and "spoke harshly to them" (Genesis 42:7). He also took his brother Simeon and had him "bound before their eyes" (v. 24). Simeon remained jailed until a second trip (necessary because their grain had run out) brought Benjamin and the remaining brothers to Egypt. Eventually, Joseph revealed himself to his stunned brothers who were "terrified at his presence" (45:3). Obviously, they assumed that all these years Joseph had been nursing a grudge against them, and Joseph's treatment of Simeon certainly confirmed their suspicions.

Joseph quickly made known that he had no such intentions to harm his brothers. "Then he threw his arms around his brother Benjamin and wept. . . . And he kissed all his brothers and wept over them" (vv. 14-15).

His brothers, however, were still not ready to believe that Joseph had forgiven them. After their father died, they had a meeting without Joseph to discuss this issue: "What if Joseph holds a grudge against us and pays us back for all the wrongs we did to him?" (50:15) Anew, they asked Joseph to forgive them: "Please forgive the sins of the servants of the God of your father" (v. 17). Joseph wept when he received this message, perhaps out of sadness that his brothers had not fully understood that he had already forgiven them but also perhaps because for the first time they had requested his forgiveness. His response had to be comforting to them:

Don't be afraid. Am I in the place of God? You intended to harm me, but God intended it for good to accomplish what is now being done, the saving of many lives. So then, don't be afraid. I will provide for you and your children (vv. 19-21).

In this case study, we see Joseph, as prime minister of Egypt, modeling the three facets of forgiveness: (1) he did not, once he forgave his brothers, keep raising the issue again; (2) he did not, once he had forgiven his brothers, go around telling others about all the bad things his brothers had done to him. Indeed, he must have said good things because the Pharaoh responded with an invitation for the whole family to relocate in Egypt; and (3) he did not, once he had extended forgiveness, dwell on the matter himself.

The second case study is the Parable of the Lost Son found in Luke 15:11-32. In this story, a businessman (presumably a farmer · because he had hired servants and had ready access to a fatted calf) had two sons. The younger one knew that eventually he would be getting a large inheritance, but was unwilling to wait. So the father divided the estate between them. The older son kept his part, and presumably invested it. But the younger son "set off for a distant country and there squandered his wealth in wild living" (15:13). In desperation, the younger son hired himself out to a pig farmer and often, because of his intense hunger, settled for pig food as his own. Finally, he came to his senses and began to realize that he would have been better off at home as a hired hand of his father. So he planned his "I'm sorry, Dad," speech and set off for home prepared for anything, but hoping for the best.

118

Back at the father's house, the older brother was feeling pretty good. Little brother was finally out of the picture and he had little brother to thank for the fact that now he had his inheritance also. His father, however, must have anxiously awaited for some word of how his younger son was doing. Apparently, he was so eager for him to return home that one of the standing assignments of the hired servants was to keep an ongoing lookout for this son. Was the father disappointed that his younger son had left home? Probably. Was the father upset that his son would probably do exactly what he ended up doing? Presumably. Was the father holding a grudge against this son, unwilling to set things right until he apologized? Obviously not. The text, illustrating the earlier point that both the offended and the offender have a responsibility to make things right, indicates that as the son approached home ("while he was still a long way off," v. 20), the father saw him and was filled with compassion. Interestingly, the wording reflects the similar response given by Joseph to his brothers: "He ran to his son, threw his arms around him and kissed him." All was forgiven.

The father was so pleased the lost son had returned that he hosted a party, showering the returned prodigal with a new wardrobe, shoes, and matching jewelry. Indeed, restoration was full.

One person in the story, however, was not willing to forgive. Even though the older brother had already received his share of the property, he apparently thought that because he had not gone out and squandered it, as did his younger brother, that the younger brother should have to reflect "fruits of repentance" before he deserved forgiveness. In essence, the older brother believed that the father, with regard to the younger son, had forgiven too quickly, if not foolishly.

CONCLUSION

We have learned several key truths from this discussion about forgiveness. First, as forgiven persons, leaders need to *be* forgiving persons. Second, the responsibility for initiating forgiveness is on both the one offended and the offender. Third, leaders have the responsibility to extend forgiveness when it is requested. They don't have the option to refuse to grant it. Fourth, even when one repeats the same offense against the leader over and over, the leader is still under a biblical mandate to forgive. Finally, adverse spiritual consequences follow one's failure to extend forgiveness—specifically, Christ will not forgive the "unforgiving" person's sins.

As stated earlier, given the leader's number of contacts, the competing demands from his or her various constituencies, and the overall leadership focus required, the leader who is unwilling to forgive will struggle in leadership. Indeed, the effective leader must always be characterized by a forgiving spirit. Failure to reflect this attitude, as difficult as it may be to do in both word and deed, produces negative results for leadership.

Charles Colson tells the terrifying story of Nazi war criminal Adolf Eichmann and his first meeting with the concentration camp survivor Yehiel Dinur, who testified against Eichmann at the Nuremburg trials. As Colson tells the story, when the two saw each other for the first time, "Dinur began to sob uncontrollably, then fainted, collapsing in a heap on the floor. . . . Was Dinur overcome by hatred? Fear? Horrid memories? No; it was none of these. Rather, as Dinur explained . . . all at once he realized Eichmann was not the godlike army officer who had sent so many to their deaths. This Eichmann was an ordinary man. 'I was afraid about myself . . . I saw that I am capable to do this. I am . . . exactly like he.' "[1] As Colson observes, "For as a result of the Fall, sin is in each of us—not just the susceptibility to sin, but sin itself."[2] Concludes Colson, "Dinur, the Auschwitz survivor, is right—Eichmann is in us, each of us. But until we can face that truth, dreadful as it may be, cheap grace and lukewarm faith—the hallmarks of ungrateful hearts—will continue to abound in a crippled church."[3]

To paraphrase Colson: until we see that, as leaders, we have the capacity to commit the same sin committed by ones seeking our forgiveness, we will not readily be good forgivers. God help us, as leaders, to forgive even as Christ has forgiven us.

PERSPECTIVE, PLANNING, AND LEADERSHIP[1]

Some variables of leadership, including those presented elsewhere in this book, enhance the leadership role. Their absence, however, is not necessarily fatal to the enterprise. The leader who fails to possess proper *perspective*, however, will struggle. Perspective is tied directly to several things, including vision and planning. As John White notes:

> People do not follow programs, but leaders who inspire them. They act when a vision stirs in them a reckless hope of something greater than themselves, hope of fulfillment they had never before dared to aspire to.[2]

In this chapter, we start with a Bible account that involves perspective, move on to some thoughts about planning, then close with another Bible account which illustrates these concepts.

Numbers 13 describes how the Children of Israel continued their slow progress toward occupying the Promised Land. Having taken an extraordinarily long time to get to that point in the journey, Moses didn't want any foul-ups. So he appointed a group of fact finders (spies) to go into the Promised Land and to bring back their assessment of what lay before them. His instructions were as follows:

See what the land is like and whether the people who live

there are strong or weak, few or many. What kind of land do they live in? Is it good or bad? What kind of towns do they live in? Are they unwalled or fortified? How is the soil? Is it fertile or poor? Are there trees on it or not? (Numbers 13:18-20)

As the story developed and the spies returned home, they ended up giving a "mixed report." The majority of the fact finders made the following observations:

We went into the land to which you sent us, and it does flow with milk and honey! Here is its fruit. But the people who live there are powerful, and the cities are fortified and very large. We even saw descendants of Anak [the giant] there (Numbers 13:27-28).

The minority report, filed by Caleb and Joshua, had a different focus:

The land we passed through and explored is exceedingly good. If the Lord is pleased with us, he will lead us into that land, a land flowing with milk and honey, and will give it to us. Only do not rebel against the Lord. And do not be afraid of the people of the land, because we will swallow them up. Their protection is gone, but the Lord is with us. Do not be afraid of them (Numbers 14:7).

In essence, the majority said, "Wow, what a terrific place! But how can we ever handle the price it will cost us to secure it? Indeed, we can't." The minority said something to this effect: "Wow, what a terrific place! The cost to secure it may be steep, but with God's help we can do it."

Which side was right? Both had seen the exact same things. Yet why did the majority give a negative report and the minority such a positive one? In organizations of all sizes, with persons presumably viewing the "same" set of facts, more times than not, leaders are faced with a majority and a minority report. How does the leader know which one is the correct analysis?

I'd like to suggest that in the story of the spies, one reason for the difference in viewpoint was godly perspective. One side saw the situation from only man's perspective while the other side saw the situation from God's perspective. Having a godly perspective is absolutely critical to leadership, because at times a situation looks absolutely hopeless from a human standpoint. But just how does a leader go about getting a biblical perspective on a given situation?

PERSPECTIVE AND GOAL-SETTING

First, leaders must start with God-given goals. What is it that God desires for the organization He has called me to lead? Does He want more buildings? More members? More students? More endowment? Does He want improved character in the persons associated with the organization? These and other questions are the beginning points in the search for biblical perspective.

Many times Christian organizations set their own goals. Then God is asked to bless them. In the case of Moses and the spies, the key to knowing which report was the proper one was a clear understanding of God's goals for the organization. With these goals clearly in mind, discernment of other matters came much more easily.

Caleb and Joshua were able to see the situation from God's perspective for several reasons. First, they understood that God was going to give them the Promised Land: "He will lead us into that land . . . and will give it to us" (13:8). Further, they understood that God would be their protection and would be with them: "Their protection is gone, but the Lord is with us. Do not be afraid of them" (v. 9). In brief, though they had seen the same walls and giants, their outlook was influenced more by the promises of God and their understanding of how God had previously worked in history. If that were not so, they too would have struggled with the right perspective.

In the pursuit of the proper perspective, the leader must be diligent in the search for God-given goals. Without such vision, the perspective will be missing and the people will perish—something that indeed happened to the Children of Israel who refused to view the Promised Land situation with the right perspective. Godly perspective, then, is related to God-given goals.

Further, *the leader must surround himself with persons who share this same commitment to God-given goals.* As we together, then, grapple with what ought to be the God-given goals of the

123

organization, the Spirit of God is able to make clear what He intends for us to accomplish—together. In my search for perspective, this must be my starting place. I will seldom be able to effectively understand or ascertain God-given goals if I am insensitive or out of tune with God-given purposes for both myself and the organization.

In addition, the beginning points for these kinds of goals ought always be the achievement of the goals God has for me personally—goals such as reflecting the fruit of the Spirit in my life and refusing to abandon my "first love" (see Revelation 2:4). Until this kind of Christlike influence pervades every fiber of my being, I will fail to grasp a situation through His eyes.

PERSPECTIVE AND PLANNING

Secondly, good planning helps provide proper perspective. Leaders must commit themselves and their organizations to developing a good planning process. Too many Christian organizations see planning as a waste of time. "Why plan?" they argue. "We can't predict the future. Besides, Scripture tells us to 'take no thought for the morrow.' Furthermore, planning takes away time that could be better used in the organization." Really?

We need to recognize that some sort of organizational planning is unavoidable. The question is whether leaders will affect the future with purpose or at random. Both Paul (Romans 6:15-23) and Peter (2 Peter 2:19) suggest that people are slaves to that which masters and controls them. While professing freedom from slavery of one type, we can become victims of another. The same is true of planning. While professing freedom from the bondage of planning, we can become enslaved to the tyranny of the results of not planning.

What's more, *planning ought to be seen as a legitimate function of biblical stewardship.* Those who work within any organization, Christian or secular, work with three key resources—money, abilities, and time. Scripture has a lot to say about each of these. With regard to money and possessions, Jesus taught, "Whoever can be trusted with very little can also be trusted with much, and whoever is dishonest with very little will be dishonest with much" (Luke 16:10). With regard to abilities, Paul wrote extensively about those skills and gifts bestowed on every believer. We read in 1 Corinthians 4:2, for example, "Those who have been given a trust must prove faithful." Finally, regarding the proper use of time, Proverbs 18:9 tells us, "One who is slack in his work is brother to one who destroys." As followers of Christ, we believe that we have a stewardship responsibility for all the resources that God has given to us. In brief, we believe we cannot practice good stewardship unless our planning helps us make the most of our resources.

Exhortations relating to stewardship appear throughout Scripture (each of the following quotations is from *The Living Bible*):

> The wise man looks ahead. The fool attempts to fool himself and won't face facts (Proverbs 14:8).

> Plans go wrong with too few counselors; many counselors bring success (Proverbs 15:22).

> What a shame—yes, how stupid!—to decide before knowing the facts! (Proverbs 18:13)

> Don't go ahead with your plans without the advice of others (Proverbs 20:18).

> Any enterprise is built by wise planning, becomes strong through common sense, and profits wonderfully by keeping abreast of the facts (Proverbs 24:3-4).

> A sensible man watches for problems ahead and prepares to meet them. The simpleton never looks, and suffers the consequences (Proverbs 27:12).

With these observations providing some background, what follows are several guidelines for planning.

1. *Planning must reflect previously established goals.* If it doesn't matter where we want to end up, we can take any road to get there. Similarly, we can always hit the target if we draw it after we take the shot. The point is that if we want to affect the future with purpose, we need to set goals. Ezra, for example, had a goal to "seek the law of the Lord, and to do it, and to teach in Israel statutes and judgments" (Ezra 7:10, KJV). Christ knew that His goal was "to save that which was lost" (Matthew 18:11, KJV). Paul was committed to "press toward the mark for the prize of the high calling of God in Christ Jesus" (Philippians 3:14, KJV). These

125

people had goals which they diligently pursued. We should do the same in our planning.

2. *Priorities must be developed among given goals.* Scripture points out that all choices are not equally worthy of praise. The psalmist, for example, notes that the Lord "helps me do what honors him the most" (Psalm 23:3, TLB). And David shares with us another of his priorities in Psalm 27:4: "The one thing I want from God, the thing I seek most of all, is the privilege of meditating in his Temple, living in his presence every day of my life, delighting in his incomparable perfections and glory" (TLB). In short, part of the goal-setting process for leaders is developing priorities among desired goals.

3. *Planning requires knowledge of the facts as they exist and not as we wish them.* This point has been made in our previous references from Proverbs. An illustration might be helpful. If we want to go to Los Angeles (our goal), our plan for getting there will depend, among other things, on where we are in relationship to our goal. Getting to Los Angeles will require different tactics if we're living in Portland, Oregon than if we're living in Portland, Maine. Where we are in relationship to our given goal is part of the fact-gathering process and is essential in developing our plans.

4. *Planning doesn't discount the past but is definitely future-oriented.* One of the fears of planning expressed by many is that it ultimately abandons the past, with all of its rich traditions and memories. We would argue to the contrary that proper planning doesn't abandon the past—indeed, it's *built* on the past. On the other hand, planning does not elevate the past or worship it. As was noted earlier, planning is definitely future-oriented. One of the best examples of this balance can be found in Paul's letter to the Philippians. Paul had accomplished much in his life, yet his attitude was "forgetting what is behind and straining toward what is ahead" (Philippians 3:13).

In brief, we believe that for any Christian organization planning is a biblically endorsed function and process which leads not only to improved stewardship of available resources, but also to the accomplishment of goals. These goals reflect the tasks God has given us. In saying this, the leader must be aware that "the Lord builds the house" (Psalm 127:1) and that "we can make our plans, but the final outcome is in God's hands" (Proverbs 16:1,

TLB; cf. James 4:13-16). What one hopes for in planning is expressed so eloquently by David in Psalm 20:4-5 (TLB):

> May [God] grant you your heart's desire and fulfill all your plans. May there be shouts of joy when we hear the news of your victory, flags flying with praise to God for all that he has done for you. May he answer all your prayers!

I want to reiterate that unless there is a willingness to face facts, planning will not work. Planning is the process of determining how I get from where I am to where I want to go. Without goals, I can't plan. Without self-assessment, I can't plan.

Back to Joshua and Caleb. They had their goal clearly in view—they were to go into the Promised Land. They were abreast of the facts. And because they understood God's goals and because they were relying on God's strength for their victory, they put a much different emphasis on the facts than did the others. Their plan was to go forward and conquer the land.

PERSPECTIVE AND THE COUNSEL OF OTHERS

We could not conclude our analysis of this matter of perspective without asking, "To whom does the leader listen when he or she receives conflicting advice?" While no one rule is suggested, leaders must remember that the majority is not always correct. Nor is the minority, for that matter. The leader, then, must carefully discern between those recommendations which are more correct than others. Majority rule is never a good substitute for proper analysis and discernment by the leader.

Let's look again at the story of Nehemiah, one we've discussed in part earlier in this book.

Having been impressed with the need (i.e., the terrible conditions in Jerusalem), his first response to this bad news was to do nothing—except *weep, fast, and pray* for several days. His prayer to the Lord is recorded in Nehemiah 1 and in it he reminds God of the previous promises He made to His people:

> Remember the instruction you gave your servant Moses, saying, "If you are unfaithful, I will scatter you among the nations, but if you return to me and obey my commands,

then even if your exiled people are at the farthest horizon, I will gather them from there and bring them to the place I have chosen as a dwelling for my Name" (Nehemiah 1:8-9).

Some additional time elapsed before he felt ready to *take further action* on behalf of Jerusalem.

It is clear, at least from this part of the account, that Nehemiah felt strongly about the need for reflective leadership—that is, leadership wherein listening to that still small voice becomes a priority. Leaders sometimes are guilty of reacting too quickly to a crisis or an opportunity. This leader was patient with his time so that he would know the mind of God in the matter.

Four months later, the king one day noticed Nehemiah's downcast demeanor and wanted to know what was wrong. After a quick prayer to God, Nehemiah told the king about the rebuilding project necessary at Jerusalem. The king agreed to a leave of absence for Nehemiah, supplied him with building materials, letters of safe passage, and a security force (Nehemiah 2:1-10).

Thus far, Nehemiah had a clear sense of God's call to move forward with the rebuilding project. He did not know the extent of the repairs needed, however. When Nehemiah got to Jerusalem, he did his own, private *assessment of what needed to be done*:

I went to Jerusalem, and after staying there three days I set out during the night with a few men. I had not told anyone what my God had put in my heart to do for Jerusalem. There were no mounts with me except the one I was riding on. . . . The officials did not know where I had gone or what I was doing, because as yet I had said nothing to the Jews or the priests or nobles or officials or any others who would be doing the work (Nehemiah 2:11-12, 16).

It was only after the need had been assessed that Nehemiah was able to develop a plan. He knew *others needed to be involved in the task*. It's important to note that he didn't start by issuing orders to the people. Rather, he shared with them how God had been working in his life and the kind of support which had been given him by the king:

Then I said to them, "You see the trouble we are in: Jerusalem lies in ruins, and its gates have been burned with fire. Come, let us rebuild the wall of Jerusalem, and we will no longer be in disgrace" (Nehemiah 2:17).

Eventually, and not without outside opposition as well as infighting, the wall was constructed. Nehemiah was quick to recognize the fact that God was the reason *the work was completed*:

So the wall was completed on the twenty-fifth of Elul, in fifty-two days. When all our enemies heard about this and all the surrounding nations saw it, our enemies lost their self-confidence, because they realized that this work had been done with the help of our God (Nehemiah 6:15-16).

Note again the importance of perspective. Nehemiah could have gotten discouraged with the immensity of the task. But instead he was able to see the project as being achievable and then to see it through to completion because his perspective was informed by a total dependence upon the Lord. He had a clear sense of God-given goals; his plans were based on a fair assessment of the need; and the plan, despite opposition, was carried out.

In Nehemiah's life, and in the life of every leader, proper (i.e., God-given) perspective can make a significant difference. While the organization will not in itself achieve its potential only because the leader has perspective, in all likelihood, the leader who lacks perspective will seldom help the organization move purposefully forward.

EXCELLENCE AND LEADERSHIP

The word *excellence* **is linked to everything** from books and beverages to ball clubs and banks. As one writer has put it:

> Excellence is "in"! It is now fashionable to be excellent. Corporations, colleges, and football coaches proclaim their commitment to excellence, while television extravaganzas celebrate what they claim to be examples of excellence. . . . Everyone loves excellence and shuns mediocrity.[1]

Just what is excellence or even Christian excellence? Does it differ from the concept of success? Does it have relevance to leaders of Christian organizations? If so, in what ways? These questions are crucial and it's to their discussion that I now turn.

EXCELLENCE REVISITED

In recent years probably nothing has done more to trigger widespread discussion of the term *excellence* than the popular business book by Peters and Waterman, *In Search of Excellence.*[2] To be sure, the book has a number of interesting points. For instance, I like its emphasis on process and people, items which are readily reflected in the book's eight basic principles. I say a hearty "amen" to its observation that "the real role of the chief executive is to manage the values of the organization."[3] The concept of "management by wandering around" is one that an effective leader is advised to pursue.

As much as I enjoyed reading this book, however, it appears to have several significant shortcomings. For example, the authors don't really define what they mean by excellence. My sense is that they are using the term *excellence* to be synonymous with the term *success*, and success is defined in fairly straightforward terms—higher profits and better products. In Peters and Waterman's view, by following eight basic steps, a company will be more capable of achieving the kind of success it desires. In essence, these steps become means to the ends of excellence and success—the epitome of corporate achievement. In this domain, excellence has a single dimension that must be served. Obviously, this is not necessarily wrong, because all of us have pursued this kind of "achievement excellence" through accomplished goals—the achievement of a college degree sufficing as but one example.

John Gardner is another who has written extensively on this subject of excellence. In his books *Excellence*[4] and *Self-Renewal*[5] Gardner tends to take a somewhat broader view of the concept of excellence and suggests that it exists in all facets of our society and in a variety of ways.

> There are many varieties of excellence.... In the intellectual field alone there are many kinds of excellence. There is the kind of intellectual activity that leads to a new theory and the kind that leads to a new machine. There is the mind that finds its most effective expression in teaching and the mind that is most at home in research. There is the mind that works best in quantitative terms, and the mind that luxuriates in poetic imagery. And there is excellence in art, in music, in craftsmanship, in human relations, in technical work, in leadership, in parental responsibilities.[6]

Gardner suggests that whatever one does should be characterized by a high level of energy and technical competence. One of his more famous quotes in this regard illustrates the point:

> An excellent plumber is infinitely more admirable than an incompetent philosopher. The society which scorns excellence in plumbing because plumbing is a humble activity and tolerates shoddiness in philosophy because it is an

exalted activity will have neither good plumbing nor good philosophy. Neither its pipes nor its theories will hold water.[7]

Gardner makes several other substantive observations which I believe are useful for this discussion. First, he suggests that there can be no excellence without standards:

> Our society cannot achieve greatness unless individuals at many levels of ability accept the need for high standards of performance and strive to achieve those standards within the limits possible for them. . . . We cannot have islands of excellence in a sea of slovenly indifference to standards.[8]

Inrig argues correctly, in my opinion, that setting "excellence as the standard is not enough. What is the standard of excellence? How do we identify and measure it?"[9] Discerning the relationship between standards and excellence seems to be one of our primary tasks. We not only have to grapple with the concept of standards in our personal lives (e.g., level of degrees sought after, physical fitness, involvement with family, etc.), but we also have to grapple with it in an organizational setting (e.g., do all personnel, for example, require the same degree of rigor in pursuing excellence in a given task?) Probably many of us can remember experiencing at one time or another during our student days the sense that "I'd rather have a B from her than a A from him." This search for standards, particularly in the context of the Christian organization, must be one of the most important concerns for leaders. Do we put our emphasis on externals or input standards (e.g., quality of staff, dollars raised), or do we focus on output standards (e.g., number of people served, etc.)?

Two cautions are in order. First, leaders need to beware of searching only for "either/or" solutions because our emphasis should include both types of standards—input and output. Second, leaders must not avoid such a search simply because of its degree of difficulty. Indeed, leaders must be careful not to confuse the "degree of difficulty" and "degree of impossibility." In this regard, Gardner suggests:

> We accept all kinds of shoddy education that is no more

than going through the motions. We pretend that so many courses, so many credits, so many hours in a classroom, so many books add up to an education. . . . We seem immensely satisfied with the outer husk of the enterprise—the number of dollars spent, the size of laboratories, the number of people involved, the fine projects outlined, the number of publications. Why do we grasp so desperately at externals? Partly because . . . it is easier to organize the external aspects of things. The mercurial spirit of great teaching and great scholarship cannot be organized, rationalized, delegated or processed. The formalities and externals can.[10]

We must certainly guard against assuming that because certain externals or input standards are present that the standard of excellence is satisfied.

Finally, Gardner's description of the self-renewing organization reflects many of the same characteristics of Peters and Waterman's excellent company—"loose in procedure, unclear in organizational lines, variable in policies."[11]

To summarize where we've gone thus far, Peters and Waterman see success in the context of a corporate dimension using excellence as a means to that end. Excellence is primarily seen as achievement. If it is excellent, it is a success. Gardner sees excellence as both means and ends, based on high standards and characterized by self-renewal.

Turning from these efforts, which are generally characteristic of the literature in this area, I also want to consider several recent books on excellence published by book houses of an evangelical stripe. In *The Success Fantasy*,[12] Campolo argues that worldly success generally means wealth, power, and prestige with all of its perjorative trappings. He sees this type of success as inconsistent with the teachings of Scripture. Robert Sandin's *The Search for Excellence*,[13] while not defining excellence or clearly stating standards, implies that excellence in Christian higher education in particular is characterized by certain external standards. In listing "bench marks of quality" he includes items such as an institution's finances, its library, instructional and physical resources, and concludes that colleges with less of these kinds of things, "are . . . less prepared to meet the educational and economic competition of our times."[14]

Two of the more helpful Christian books on this topic are Inrig's *A Call to Excellence*[15] and Johnston's *Christian Excellence.*[16] Inrig notes that excellence is a multidimensional concept that great thinkers have approached from several diverse perspectives. *Social excellence* involves the proper pursuit of talents and achievements that have social utility.[17] *Human excellence* involves the development of man or woman as human.[18] *Personal excellence* reflects the psychological jargon of the self-actualization seekers so prevalent in our narcissistic culture. *Utilitarian excellence* is the pursuit of those things that are external ends, such as material possessions or public notoriety.[20] Finally, Inrig discusses *technical excellence* as levels of skills whether in music, art, science, athletics, etc.[21] He ends up suggesting that excellence for the Christian should focus more on qualities of character represented by the fruit of the Spirit and other such spiritual traits than on pursuing the more worldly, achievement-oriented definitions of excellence.

Johnston juxtaposes success with excellence and argues that Christians ought to be pursuing excellence, not success. For him, "Success is attaining cultural goals . . . and . . . is reserved mostly for those who have made or who are making it big. These people wear clothing with the right labels, eat at the best restaurants. . . ."[22] Whereas success is reserved for only the few, excellence can be achieved by everybody. The differences between success and excellence for Johnston are obvious:

> *Success* bases our worth on a comparison with others. *Excellence* gauges our value by measuring us against our own potential. *Success* grants its rewards to the few but is the dream of the multitudes. *Excellence* is available to all living beings but is accepted by the . . . few. *Success* focuses its attention on the external—becoming the tastemaker for the insatiable appetites of the . . . consumer. *Excellence* beams its spotlight on the internal spirit. . . . *Success* encourages expedience and compromise, which prompts us to treat people as means to our ends. *Excellence* cultivates principles and consistency. . . ."[23]

Whereas Inrig sees excellence as characterized by qualities such as the fruit of the Spirit, Johnston's metaphor is *agape* love.

EXCELLENCE AND SUCCESS IN SCRIPTURE

Success is not viewed as a dirty word in Scripture. In fact, on a number of occasions people were promised success if they remained true to God. For example, God promised Joshua success and prosperity if he followed certain biblical guidelines. Clearly, the kind of success Joshua experienced reflects achievement in the best sense of the word.

First, Joshua achieved military success. He had the kind of reputation with his people that many leaders never experience, for it is written: "That day the Lord exalted Joshua in the sight of all Israel; and they revered him all the days of his life, just as they had revered Moses" (Joshua 4:14).

Joshua was also successful materially, for later we read: "When they had finished dividing the land into its allotted portions, the Israelites gave Joshua son of Nun an inheritance among them, as the Lord had commanded. They gave him the town he asked for—Timnath Serah in the hill country of Ephraim. And he built up the town and settled there" (Joshua 19:49-50).

Many leaders would value what was said of the organization under Joshua's leadership—Israel—to be said of their own leadership efforts:

> So the Lord gave Israel all the land he had sworn to give their forefathers, and they took possession of it and settled there. The Lord gave them rest on every side, just as he had sworn to their forefathers. Not one of their enemies withstood them; the Lord handed all their enemies over to them. Not one of all the Lord's good promises to the house of Israel failed; every one was fulfilled (Joshua 21:43-45).

Joshua achieved success because it was given to him by the Lord. He achieved success because he was committed to doing God's work God's way. He was careful to obey the Lord's command laid out at the beginning of his leadership career: "Do not let this Book of the Law depart from your mouth; meditate on it day and night, so that you may be careful to do everything written in it. Then you will be prosperous and successful" (Joshua 1:8).

In addition to these references to success in the Book of Joshua, Scripture also speaks of excellence. The psalmist, for example, notes that God's name and lovingkindness are excellent:

> O Lord our Lord, how excellent is thy name in all the earth!
> Who hast set thy glory above the heavens. . . . O Lord our
> Lord, how excellent is thy name in all the earth! (Psalm 8:1,
> 9; KJV)

> How excellent is thy lovingkindness, O God! therefore the
> children of men put their trust under the shadow of thy
> wings (Psalm 36:7, KJV).

Elsewhere in the Old Testament, we are challenged to reflect
excellence in our speech: "Excellent speech becometh not a fool:
much less do lying lips a prince" (Proverbs 17:7, KJV).

One of the major references to excellence in the New Testament is 1 Corinthians 13. In 1 Corinthians 12 the Apostle Paul has
been discussing the matter of spiritual gifts. He attempts to show
that in the body of Christ there is a variety of gifts, that each one
is vitally needed for the body to properly function, and that no
one gift ought to be sought above the others for the sole reason of
having higher status than another believer. He then concludes this
discourse with this exhortation: "But eagerly desire the greater
gifts. And now I will show you the most excellent way" (1 Corinthians 12:31).

And what constituted Paul's most excellent way? His answer
is found in 1 Corinthians 13, where he sets forth the character
qualities of Christian excellence. Many times the Christian leader
is tempted to read 1 Corinthians 13:1-3 as follows:

> When I speak with the tongues of men and of angels, I am
> smooth sounding and sought after to be a major Christian
> conference speaker and to put out my own, copyrighted film
> series. When I have the gift of prophecy and understand all
> mysteries and have a lot of knowledge and so much faith
> that I can remove mountains, I write books, speak at proph-
> ecy conferences, and do healing seminars. When I give away
> all my earthly goods to feed the poor and when I willingly
> endanger my life for the sake of the Gospel, then I'll be given
> honorary degrees, elected to the boards of several Christian
> organizations, and perhaps have a building named in my
> honor.

Obviously, that is not at all what Paul has in mind. What he does appear to be saying is that if I, as a leader, have all of the positive qualities identified in verses 1-3, but fail to couple with them the qualities of Christian love in action, I have failed to understand what Christian excellence is all about.

Not content to make his point on Christian excellence only in his first letter to the Corinthians, he hammers it home again in his letter to the Philippians: "That ye may approve things that are excellent; that ye may be sincere and without offense till the day of Christ" (Philippians 1:10).

It appears to be a fair reading of both texts that Paul was concerned that his readers, including leaders, would settle for the good things when he wanted them to aspire to the best things, the excellent things.

Interestingly, none of Paul's comments about excellence bears any resemblance to the definition of success as achievement found in the Old Testament, particularly those references we identified in Joshua. The success motif in the Old Testament seems to be associated with the kind of excellence discussed by Peters and Waterman in their book, *In Search of Excellence*. The standard of excellence seen in the New Testament is a qualitative one, one that addresses more the issue of how one lives than how much one accumulates.

THE LEADER AND EXCELLENCE

Thus far in this chapter we have examined excellence from several viewpoints: those of secular literature, Christian literature, and the Bible itself. Now we ask the question, "How then might a Christian leader pursue excellence in leadership?" Four areas are suggested.

1. *Leaders need to pursue excellence in the quality of their preparation.* It is true that God has chosen to use all sorts of people to do His work throughout the ages of time, and that many of them did not seem to have the preparation the management types of today would deem essential. Persons such as Gideon come readily to mind, whose preparation seemed primarily of the heart.

But in other cases God put His future leadership choices through an extended period of preparation. Joseph and Moses are but two examples.

From his youth Joseph felt that God had called him to be a

leader. Indeed, he was so outspoken about this calling that his father admonished him to quit talking about it so much. But leadership did not come early or easily for Joseph. During his teens and twenties, hard circumstances befell him in order to prepare him for his future role. Joseph was educated in cisterns, the slave market, and finally, in prison. Hardly a course of development to suggest to anyone who wants to be a senior-level government official.

Yet while Joseph was being prepared for a subsequent leadership assignment, we note two curious observations. First, we find no evidence that Joseph was dissatisfied with God's conditions of preparation for leadership. Second, we see no evidence that Joseph tried to accelerate God's timetable.

In the first instance, we don't see Joseph constantly complaining about all of the hardships that God brought his way. There is no evident animosity toward his brothers, no bitterness about the oppressive conditions of Egyptian slavery, no complaining about the deplorable state of the prison. Indeed, Joseph exhibited a disquieting contentedness about his circumstances. It was as if Joseph knew that God had something better up ahead and that his responsibility, during the difficult moments in the meantime, was to concentrate on being obedient to God.

What's more, it appears that Joseph was content not only with his conditions but also with God's timing. We don't see him forcing God's hand. He could have yielded to the seducing charms of Potiphar's wife in order to advance his lot in life, especially since he probably knew refusal of her request meant prison. He could have complained when the cupbearer forgot to mention his special abilities to the Pharaoh. Through it all he faithfully waited.

It must be noted that Joseph *did* take advantage of opportunities that God presented. For example, we know he disliked the Egyptian prison because of his request to the cupbearer—"mention me to Pharaoh and get me out of this prison" (Genesis 40:14). Yet when his request went unhonored, he didn't get angry at God. Further, we must note that Pharaoh never asked Joseph what solutions should be considered to resolve the coming famine that Joseph had just predicted. Joseph simply saw his chance and must have said something like, "While I have the floor, let me tell you some of the ways you might deal with this problem." The rest is biblical history. Joseph, in God's time, became the functional prime minister of Egypt. He was ready, at God's call, and over the span of several days, to go from prisoner to prime minister.

How unlike Joseph are many contemporary Christian leaders. Whether pastor or college president, maneuvering is heavy and calculated to get the right college or the right church. There is a keen awareness that "if I'm stuck in this hole for too long, I'll never be able to serve at a really good church or college." Furthermore, not only is there maneuvering to get the right position (translated—be in the right conditions so that I can be promotable), but there is also the maneuvering to get the right position at the right time. The thinking goes something like this: "I'm fifty and I've got one more move left, so if I don't pursue this new option now, I might as well forget it."

Yet, as we see with Joseph, God may have something for us to learn about both His conditions of preparation as well as His time of preparation. Being sensitive to His leadership in these areas, and truly content with where we are right now, are ways we can model excellence in leadership.

Let's consider next how God prepared Moses for leadership. Some writers have suggested that Moses' life can be thought of in three periods of approximately forty years each—forty years as one of Egypt's best and brightest; forty years as a caretaker of sheep; and forty years as a shepherd of God's people.

Moses' early years would be viewed by many as a proper preparation for leadership. Educated in the best schools of Egypt, and as the son of Pharaoh's daughter, he had it made. By our standards he would have been a graduate of Harvard. As Stephen noted, "Moses was educated in the wisdom of the Egyptians and was powerful in speech and action" (Acts 7:22). In brief, he was on the way to being fantastically successful.

Yet God had other plans involving Moses' preparation for His leadership. God's plan included Moses' abandoning the good life he had in Egypt, shepherding in the wilderness, then wandering in the desert with a rebellious and stubborn people. The irony of this leadership saga is that, even after all of these painful experiences, God told Moses he could neither go into nor enjoy the Promised Land. Further, at the time God took his life, "his eyes were not weak nor his strength gone" (Deuteronomy 34:7). Moses appeared to be content with both the circumstances and the timing God gave him to contend with.

I believe God wants leaders who diligently work at achieving excellence in the quality of their preparation, whether through degrees or experience. But we see from these two examples of biblical leaders that preparation for leadership involves more than degrees or position. It also involves contentedness in circumstances and an awareness that God's timing is never late. Striving to lead in the big church or to serve as president of the famous university may not be evidence of impure motives. Forcing God's timetable, coupled with an attitude of discontent while serving the smaller out-of-the-way organization, most assuredly may.

2. *Leaders need to pursue excellence in qualities reflecting Christian character.* Another part of this book will explore more in depth the devotional life of the leader. This section deals with how the leader might encourage the development of excellent character qualities within the people who work for the organization.

First, the leader should *compliment character qualities.* In the Christian organization (where both the people within the organization and the purposes they serve are a reflection of biblical mandates), compliments regarding quality of character are far too few. Reference was earlier made to the character qualities reflected in 1 Corinthians 13. So too, the expression of excellent character qualities is found in the fruit of the Spirit: "Love, joy, peace, patience, kindness, goodness, faithfulness, gentleness and self-control" (Galatians 5:22-23).

Leaders need to reflect these qualities not only in their own lives, but they need to encourage and promote these qualities in job-related assignments. It is my strong belief that decisions regarding the initial hire, promotions, and subsequent decisions to retain an employee should take into consideration these types of character qualities as well as the other more traditional performance standards of the job. Leaders should compliment an employee's quality of self-control and/or kindness just as regularly and frequently as job performance accomplishments.

Second, the leader should *attempt to have the organization reflect the positive character qualities of its employees.* Organizations, just like people, have personalities. Churches, for example, tend to be identified as "cold" or "warm" churches. Organizations are often described with words such as "Over there they care about people"; "At that college students feel important." I believe it's possible that an organization can reflect qualities of character set forth in the fruit of the Spirit. If persons within the organization reflect these qualities, it would seem logical to assume that so too would the organization where those persons work. We go full circle then to the earlier comment—an organization's employees need to be encouraged, through the positive example of leaders, to reflect biblical qualities of character.

3. *Leaders need to pursue excellence in the organization's processes.* First, organizational procedures need to be carefully examined. Many organizational procedures go to either of two extremes. On the one hand, there may be too few procedures pertaining to how things are done. As a result, too much organizational time is spent trying to ascertain just how things should or ought to happen. Human beings are creatures of habit and some modicum of procedure can do much to contribute to a stable organizational environment. On the other hand, some organizations are too preoccupied with organizational procedures. In this kind of organization, the way things are done assumes a greater prominence than the ends sought. As Gardner notes:

> This concern for "how it is done" is also one of the diseases of which societies die. Little by little, preoccupation with method, technique and procedure gains a subtle dominance *over* the whole process of goal seeking. How it is done becomes more important than whether it is done. Means triumph over ends. Form triumphs over spirit. Method is enthroned. Men become prisoners of their procedures, and organizations that were designed to achieve some goal become obstacles in the path to that goal.[24]

Ongoing tension is guaranteed in this process/ends dialectic, but it is imperative that the leader keep such in perspective and properly manage it. As the following quote from Edith Shaeffer illustrates, the search for organizational perfection, procedurally as well as substantively, can do deadly damage to both organizations and families:

> There are no beautiful mobiles, works of art in the form of (Christian organizations) which have never been in danger

141

of being broken. Frustration, anger . . . the feeling of being misunderstood, the giving in to daydreams of perfection—these or other forms of dissatisfaction invade every organizational relationship. The difference is that the deep underlying sense of importance of (organizational) continuity must be stronger than the insistence of having perfection. People throw away what they could have by insisting on perfection which they cannot have. . . . There is a beauty in continuity which can never be had unless someone in the (organization) has the certainty that the whole art form is more important than one incident, or even a string of incidents.[25]

The process of how organizations deal with people, both within the organization and outside of it, is a critically important function of leadership. Perhaps more than any other factor, this one will do much to determine whether or not the organization will achieve excellence in its mission.

One additional emphasis is that sensitivity, sensibility, and saneness be retained as progress is made toward other types of achievement or success-oriented goals. Many times, the organizational focus on long-term results, however important those may be, tends to slant our vision of the present as somehow being less important. The goal of completing the new building or surpassing expectations on the fund-raising drive must not be pursued totally to the exclusion of present relationships, joys, or needs waiting to be met by someone—now. We must remember that one of the great "present tense" names of God is "I Am."

4. *Leaders need to pursue excellence regarding the qualities of the organizational vision.* Too few leaders give careful attention to the cultivation and nurture of the organizational dream. In a church setting, many pastors sometimes forget to emphasize to their parishioners that invitations to sing in the choir, teach a class, or help in the nursery are not more things to add to an already crowded schedule. Rather, people ought to be presented with the challenge that they have the opportunity to exercise their spiritual gifts for the good of the church; they have the opportunity to be co-laborers with God in the very important task of kingdom building. Are laborers laying bricks or building cathedrals? Are farmers pulling weeds or preparing for a harvest?

Leaders have the responsibility to cultivate vision in the organization. As Proverbs 29:18 says, "Where there is no vision, the people perish" (KJV).

Further, leaders need to cultivate dreams of excellence. This doesn't necessarily mean that the visions must always reflect bigger quantitative dimensions. A vision of excellence ought also to be replete with qualitative dimensions. It takes no greater organizational effort, furthermore, to cultivate visions of excellence than it does to promote visions of shoddiness. Perhaps just as importantly, it takes no greater effort to *achieve* visions of excellence. It is the quality of the vision that inspires the quality of the response.

CONCLUSION

Are there differences, then, with the distinctions between success and excellence in the Christian organization? While many distinctions ultimately blur, there nevertheless are differences. Christian organizations and their leaders do need to pursue success. Leaders and organizations need to have a clear set of achievable, measurable goals, calculated by organizational size and other factors. These goals must be pursued, however, only in ways that are God-honoring.

At the same time, the pursuit of excellence must encompass goals pertaining to both individual and organizational character qualities. While all Christian organizations may not be able to achieve success quantitatively (e.g., having the largest church, the best endowed college, etc.), every leader and every Christian organization can pursue excellence in terms of character qualities.

THE LEADER AS FUND-RAISER

"**I had a dream and in the dream God told me** to ask for millions of dollars to help carry out my dream." Obviously not the words of Martin Luther King, this type of "dream" is being shared by Christian leaders with the Christian public with increasing frequency. Not surprisingly, when the leader has a national media audience with whom the "dream" can be shared, the sums associated therewith take on staggering proportions. The larger the media audience, the larger the "dream," seems to be an acceptable rule of thumb.

Christian leaders nationwide are quickly jumping on the fund-raising bandwagon. To the saints who respond to their appeals, small gifts such as books, Bibles, candles, pins, and certificates are offered. More importantly to the leader, donors are "unknowingly privileged" to be placed on his mailing list.[1] To those who respond more "generously," the rewards are somewhat greater. They find their names on bricks, prayer towers, and buildings. They're invited to banquets, presented expensive plaques, given honorary degrees, and elected to institutional boards. All of these efforts are carried out in the name of Christ, and with the help of the most up-to-date technology, including automatic typewriters, word processors, and computers. John White, author of *The Golden Cow*, describes the situation:

A Christian organization feels it has to project the kind of image that will not offend those who have given for years and that at the same time will "awaken prayer interest" in a wider constituency. And image projecting calls for professional skills. One Christian leader spoke to me of the "pretty fancy footwork" needed to keep diverse supporting groups happy. A wrong sentence may cost several thousand dollars.[2]

Patti Roberts, writing in her book, *Ashes to Gold*, adds these thoughts: "We had built a wonderful machine in the name of God, and now all of our efforts were focused on keeping it running. At all costs, it must never be allowed to stop."[3]

How should the Christian who leads an organization desperate for money respond to these kinds of activities and efforts? Without a doubt, many organizations are achieving "success" using these methods.[4] Buildings are built, programs are funded, and "needs" are indeed met. Many other organizations are upgrading their fund-raising efforts in order to reap the fruits made possible by the continuing sophistication of this business. Efforts are upgraded because, "no one really knows what the financial potential of Christianity is." Are leaders to condone these efforts and activities as being ordained by God and therefore worthy of use?

Scripture provides much guidance for the leader on these difficult matters, and approaches the subject from several perspectives. Scripture offers first what can be called a *general perspective*. Second, Scripture supplies *guidance for the donor* on how he should give. Finally, Scripture provides *guidance for the leader and the organization* he represents. It is on these biblical guidelines that the balance of this chapter will be focused.

GENERAL BIBLICAL GUIDELINES

Christian biblical stewardship of financial means would appear to be an extension of an assigned stewardship for all of life. In the exercise of that stewardship, Christians are to be faithful in little things (Luke 16:10), are to seek first God's kingdom (Matthew 6:33), and as servants, should be particularly concerned about the welfare of others.

Christian teaching suggests that God ultimately is the chief donor to our organizations because "the earth is the Lord's, and the fullness thereof; the world, and they that dwell therein" (Psalm 24:1, KJV).

Since God is the owner of all, and presumably of all that anyone, Christian or otherwise, possesses, and since He is to be the focus of the Christian's actions, He should be the primary objective of all fund-raising efforts. His desire, it can be argued, requires the development of *total*—not a part-time—dependency on Him, moment by moment, day by day. He abhors an independent attitude. He asks for this dependent relationship because He bears our burdens, He loves us with an unfailing love, and He promises to supply our every need. Christians echo their collective beliefs in these principles through songs like "Day by Day," "One Day at a Time," and "What a Friend We Have in Jesus."

It may not stretch the truth of Scripture to suggest that these principles, and the others which follow, not only have an individual application but also an organizational one. This is particularly the case for the organization which aspires to be Christian. Christian organizations consist of Christian people and such organizations, arguably, ought to be accountable to the same biblical principles as are individual believers. Parenthetically, if this proposition is not accepted, then it must be concluded, among other possibilities, that the principles of Scripture lose their impact, or conversely, people can ignore them in the context of group or collective action.

BIBLICAL GUIDELINES FOR THE DONOR

First, *God is concerned that the giving of His resources to others be done with the proper intent.* A most challenging passage on this point is 1 Chronicles 29:14-17, where David provided material for the building of the temple. After he set the example in giving and others followed, he observed, "I know, my God, that you test the heart and are pleased with integrity. All these things have I *given willingly* and *with honest intent*" (1 Chronicles 29:17, italics added). Knowing why the gift is being given is an extremely important consideration for the Christian. And leaders who ask for money must likewise be careful how they ask and how they view the gift and the giver. May it never be from an impure motive or dishonest intent.

A second principle, related to the first, is that *God expects those who give of His resources to keep it quiet.* A primary passage on this point is Matthew 6:1-4. Key verses are as follows:

> So when you give to the needy, do not announce it with trumpets, as the hypocrites do in the synagogues and on the streets, to be honored by men. . . . But when you give to the needy, do not let your left hand know what your right hand is doing, so that your giving may be in secret. Then your Father, who sees what is done in secret, will reward you (vv. 2-4).

Jesus' calling attention to the widow quietly giving two coins (see Mark 12:41-44) appears to be, among other things, a worthy illustration of this guideline.

Third, *God expects those who give to do so with no expectation of a return*. In Luke 6:27-36, the Lord gave instruction on the "new" way He wanted His disciples to behave. On the topic of lending, He advised:

> And if you lend to those from whom you expect repayment, what credit is that to you? Even "sinners" lend to "sinners," expecting to be paid in full. But love your enemies, do good to them, and lend to them *without expecting to get anything back*. Then your reward will be great" (vv. 34-35, italics added).

Since the instruction is to Christians and enemies, and involves lending, and since presumably the relationship between donors and organizations is not that of an "enemy" or adversary relationship and usually involves outright gifts, not loans, the biblical guideline appears to acquire even greater force—don't give with an expectation of return!

In reviewing the many requests made for gifts, donors may be tempted to make decisions on giving based on which organization offers the biggest premium or return in exchange for the gift. A gift of a certain value yields for the donor a gift or premium which is, surprisingly, related to the size of gift. The donor gets tapes, records, books, commentaries, yes—even Bibles, if he or she properly responds to the urgings of some Christian leaders. An even more subtle example of this kind of "return on investment" philosophy is what Hales and Youngren call the "exchange relationship." The idea is that since the ministry—whether a radio station, college, church, etc.—is obviously benefiting the donor, he or she *ought* to be giving to it.[5]

Why are these exchange or premium items offered? While many "good" reasons could be given, the most obvious is that fund-raising consultants know that offering premiums or gifts to potential donors *does make a difference* in the way people respond to appeals for funds. Yet this approach may run counter to the biblical guideline of giving without expectation of return.

These guidelines for donors obviously do not constitute an entire or complete list. They do illustrate, however, some of the guidelines donors need to be sensitive to as prayerful decisions are made regarding involvement in "needy" projects.

BIBLICAL GUIDELINES FOR THE LEADER WHO ASKS

First, leaders who know that their "needy" Christian organizations are dependent on God must remember to *be content with their circumstances knowing that God has promised to supply all their needs.* For the Christian, and presumably for the leaders of Christian organizations, it appears that Scripture places a premium on contentment. The writer to the Hebrews exhorts: "Keep your lives free from the love of money and be content with what you have, because God has said, 'Never will I leave you; never will I forsake you' " (Hebrews 13:5). Paul stated that he had learned to be content "whatever the circumstances" and "in any and every situation" (Philippians 4:11-12). The secret, obviously, was that he could do all things through Christ who strengthened him (v. 13). He taught Timothy that "godliness with contentment is great gain" (1 Timothy 6:6).

Institutional contentment, as reflected in the lives of leaders, however, must also be combined with the realization that God has promised to meet *all* needs. Note the following verses:

And my God will meet all your needs according to his glorious riches in Christ Jesus (Philippians 4:19).

Put [your] hope in God, who richly provides us with everything for our enjoyment (1 Timothy 6:17).

The Lord is my shepherd, I shall lack nothing (Psalm 23:1).

Should not institutional capacities for contentment increase with an improved understanding by the leader that God is indeed in charge?

It is in this area, perhaps more than others, where Christian leaders may be overlooking biblical truth. Organizational operating assumptions, both explicit and implicit, seem to suggest that God is not capable of meeting needs, that enough is never enough, and what is really desired is for Him to meet not only needs, but also wants. White makes this observation:

> I do not know whether to be amused or saddened by the double messages Christian groups send out. The first message is: God is with us in a big way. Climb on board while you have the chance! The second message is: Something dreadful is happening. We're about to be shipwrecked on the shoals of financial need. To get both messages across at the same time calls for verbal dexterity.
>
> According to the begging mail my wife leaves on my desk, the church is in dire straits. God is apparently doing a terrific job through all the Christian organizations that write me, but he has run into a financial crisis that threatens to undo everything. In the nick of time he was saved last year because he himself prompted people to give. This year it looks as though he might not be able to make ends meet. So we must trust God and rescue him at the same time.[6]

Is it possible, as Foster suggests in *The Freedom of Simplicity*, "that sometimes God would lead us to ask for less?"[7] Howard Bowen observes that, with regard to colleges, it's difficult to determine educational costs because institutions always spend everything they take in. Other Christian organizations are not notably different in this regard. Indeed, all tend to want more, and no matter how much money was raised in the last financial campaign, there must always be another. Judging by the *ongoing* and *continuous* nature of these campaigns, is God unable to meet institutional needs, no matter how hard He tries?

If there is ever any doubt about the depths to which Christian organizations have slid, or some might consider it the heights to which they have risen, all one has to do is compare organizations' "needs lists" with the "needs lists" of those Christian brothers and sisters throughout the rest of the world. How can Christian leaders justify asking people to respond to the "need" for millions (to support employee lifestyles of big cars, houses, fancy buildings, relatively large salaries, benefit packages, etc.) when Christian brothers in Central American countries and elsewhere around the world are living with much less? How can organizations seek millions for endowments when some missions organizations barely have adequate resources for medical supplies and equipment, let alone enough for food? White describes the situation this way:

> At the heart of the matter lies our dependence upon material things. We take them for granted. We accumulate them. We go into debt to acquire them, work longer hours to earn them. They enslave us. They enslave not only our bodies but our hearts which no longer have room for the crying of the needy, the starving and the dying.
>
> Here lie the beginnings of our harlotry. We cherish our lovely buildings. We give payola to our pastors and missionaries so they will accept the spiritual responsibility that leaves us to acquire things. We take our wealth for granted while in our hearts the groans of the starving and the screams of the tortured are muted into background muzak.[8]

A second guideline for fund-raising is that *Christian leaders are not to show favoritism to the rich.* Indeed, James suggests that such favoritism is sin (James 2:1-9). Unfortunately, showing favoritism to the rich is a sin seldom mentioned by Christian leaders. Obviously *rich* is a relative term, and its definition has to be operationalized. But, however defined, this biblical mandate must be considered.

How do Christian leaders show favoritism to the rich? They do so in a variety of ways. It's not by coincidence that few boards of directors of Christian organizations have impoverished members. Banquets are held every year for their biggest donors.[9] Giving clubs are established, and buildings and sometimes institutions are named after large donors. Very few, if any, Christian organizations have a "Widow's Mite Hall." Organizations invite their largest donors to "headquarters" and try to influence people to make even larger gifts. During these visits special dinners are provided which are not the same fare provided smaller donors.

Indeed, few leaders could admit that favoritism is not in some manner shown toward the rich in order to enlist their support for "worthy" Christian endeavors.

Favoritism toward the rich manifests itself in other subtle ways. In order to make the right impression on the rich, leaders are tempted to insist on living a similar lifestyle. To use the current jargon, Christian leaders insist on going "first class" in all of their activities. Patti Roberts summarizes this problem quite succinctly:

> In order to be accepted by those who possess wealth and influence, one has to adopt at least some of the trappings of their lifestyle and that inevitably creates conflict. Jesus said we were to be servants, but it is hard to maintain a servant's heart when you dress better than 99 percent of the world. When you play golf with senators and vacation with heads of multimillion-dollar corporations, it is difficult to identify with the widow on Social Security who faithfully supports the ministry with her ten-dollar offering each month.[10]

The irony in all of this is that few wealthy donors insist on being treated better than anyone else. Most do not want to be shown favoritism or desire the publicity organizations tend to give them. Parenthetically, perhaps favoritism is shown out of a need to vicariously enjoy the donor's wealth which leaders know will never be theirs.

A third biblical guideline for fund-raising is that *Christian leaders need to have the right motive when they ask for money.* According to James 4:2-3, "You do not have, because you do not ask God. When you ask, you do not receive, because you ask with wrong motives, that you may spend what you get on your pleasures." Among other emphases, these verses suggest that asking must be proper and needs-oriented rather than wants- or pleasures-oriented.

Leaders also struggle with other proper motives in their asking. Many fund-raising efforts have as their source that of forward momentum. The thinking goes something like this. Competitor organizations A, B, and C recently launched fund-raising campaigns. If organization X doesn't soon announce some kind of campaign, their supporters may conclude that they're falling behind the others. So a campaign is launched for something—endowment will always do nicely if no more buildings are needed—in order to keep pace with the competition and to ensure continuing good public relations. Again, Patti Roberts, in assessing her involvement with a Christian organization, identifies some pitfalls in this area:

> All of our effort went to "how does this look to the public"—not "how does this look to God?" We turned our eyes to the public when we should have turned them to the wind and cried, "God, what responsibilities do we have to you?"[11]

Another reason leaders ask for support and perhaps ask amiss is to keep from losing potential gifts to other causes, including other Christian organizations. In this situation the thinking is as follows: "We have solid programs, a complete physical plant, and an endowment of $40 million. But we also know members of our constituency are now capable of making a major gift, and if we don't do something to get it, it will be lost to another cause or organization."

A third example of a potential problem in this area is what Hales and Youngren call the "hot button" mentality.[12] The theory is that a given project with a "popular" person's name will always increase the level of financial support. Usually the "hot button" project is broadly conceived. Why raise only $2 million when one knows the project or person's name is capable of generating $4 million? And if the project goal looks like it will be exceeded, additional items can be added so that all of the funds raised will appear necessary. The rule for "hot button" projects appears to be that needs can always be expanded in direct proportion to the amount of money they are capable of generating.

Care must be taken to avoid the suggestion that these three examples are *always* illustrations of asking amiss. What is suggested is that each has the *potential* of being handled in such a way that a leader ends up asking amiss. James 4:2-3 suggests that the same or greater intensity must be shown in asking God to meet needs as is shown in asking people to help with needs. The leader's task is to make sure that all projects are conceptualized and carried out with the right motive, particularly so if God is asked to bless them.

One further biblical guideline for leaders is suggested: *leaders and their organizations are not to be hoarders of money or material possessions.* Note two Scripture passages:

> Do not store up for yourselves treasures on earth. . . . But store up for yourselves treasures in heaven where moths and rust do not destroy. . . . For where your treasure is, there your heart will be also (Matthew 6:19-21).

> Command them [the rich] to do good, to be rich in good deeds, and to be generous and willing to share. In this way they will lay up treasure for themselves as a firm foundation for the coming age, so that they may take hold of the life that is truly life (1 Timothy 6:18-19).

Clearly, the instruction is to individuals, but could it not also be applied to organizations?

Several reasons for this instruction are apparent. One is that since God knows that human hearts inevitably follow treasure, they may not be focused on heaven-related matters if much treasure is held personally or is invested in human institutions.

For example, if God continuously encourages individuals with wealth to lay it up in heaven, does that commandment lose its force when the money is given to an organization such as a Christian educational institution? While not suggesting that endowment efforts are wrong in and of themselves, concern may be appropriate if institutional trust is placed in endowments rather than in a Heavenly Father's daily provision. This matter will be discussed further in the next chapter.

SUMMARY

While articles and books provide interesting observations on the topic of Christian fund-raising, the purpose of this chapter has been to suggest that the *first* source of guidance should be Scripture. As has been seen, not only are there general biblical guidelines which can be applied to fund-raising, but there also appear to be specific guidelines applicable to specific fund-raising practices. If the leader has a commitment to be responsive to *all* of Scripture, then efforts must be made to be responsive to the leadership of the Spirit of God on these matters. According to White, Scripture supports three methods of raising funds:

asking God's people for money, tent making (that is, earning your living to support your Christian service) and trusting God to supply by some means known in advance only to him. A fourth method is not scriptural: to profess to walk by faith in God above and simultaneously to hunt for funds or manipulate people into giving.[13]

Probably a favorite of many, the George Müller story illustrates a corporate application of some of the principles set forth in this chapter. Müller operated orphanages in 19th-century England, impacting thousands, using seven "unique" guidelines:

1. No funds would ever be solicited. No facts or figures concerning needs were to be revealed by the workers in the orphanage to anyone, except to God in prayer.
2. No debts would ever be incurred. The burden of experiment would therefore not be on local shopkeepers or suppliers.
3. No money contributed for a specific purpose would ever be used for any other purpose.
4. All accounts would be audited annually by professional auditors.
5. No ego-pandering by publication of donors' names, with the amount of their gifts, would be allowed; each donor would be thanked privately.
6. No "names" of prominent or titled persons would be sought for the board or to advertise the institution.
7. The success of the institution would be measured not by the numbers served or by the amounts of money taken in, but by God's blessing on the work, which Müller expected to be in proportion to the time spent in prayer.

As the story is told by Catherine Marshall, from the beginning, "George Müller and his associates stuck to their principles, spending time in prayer that ordinarily would have gone to fundraising."[14] It appears that God abundantly blessed Müller's efforts. Müller even went "first class," not only in his furnishings for each orphanage, but also in the clothing and other supplies given for the children.

Efforts must continue in the search for ways leaders might

honor the Lord through fund-raising efforts. As Christian leaders endeavor to depend on His resources, they need to learn anew the meaning of the words of Hudson Taylor: "God's work done in God's way will not lack God's supply."

HOW MUCH IS ENOUGH?

One of the issues that a leader must ultimately address is the issue of organizational growth, or, "how much is enough?" The issue is a broad one—colleges confront it on issues like number of buildings, size of endowments, and students; churches confront it on issues like number of staff, number of members, and size of facility and programs; parents confront it on issues like the size of the house, amount in savings, amount of life insurance, and lifestyle; businesses confront it on issues like size of plant, amount of product produced, and cost of services rendered. Eventually we all must decide where to draw the line.

Before this issue is explored in the context of Scripture, it must be observed that much of our desire for growth, other than a desire for growth in an intangible way, is the result of a secular mindset. Whether we like it or not, Charles Darwin has greatly influenced our thinking in this regard—even in Christian circles. Jeremy Rifkin in his book, *Algeny*, reviews the many ways social Darwinism has come to influence our thinking. Rifkin argues, persuasively in my view, that Darwin, doing nothing more than reflecting the social and economic structure of his time, 19th-century England, proceeded to rephrase that social structure in the form of a scientific-sounding theory explaining man's relation-ship to nature. As Rifkin notes:

Darwin dressed up nature with an English personality, ascribed to nature English motivations and drives, and even provided nature with an English marketplace and the English form of government. Like others who preceded him in history, Darwin borrowed from the popular culture the appropriate metaphors and then transposed them to nature, projecting a new cosmology that was remarkably similar in detail to the day-to-day life he was accustomed to.[1]

And just what were these features of day-to-day life?

The basic tenet of "Darwin's theory of the origin and development of species centered on the survival of the fittest."[2] Expressed as a "natural" principle, "in the struggle for survival, nature ensures that the strong will triumph and the weak will perish."[3] Translated into internecine competition between Christian organizations, many work overtime to develop organizational strength so that they will be the most fit of the survivors. John White puts the issue quite succinctly:

> Expansion is unthinkingly accepted among Western Christians as something good and desirable in itself. And by expansion I do not mean the spread of the gospel, but the growth of particular institutions. Expanding organizations come into conflict over money, territory and workers. At times mature thinking prevails, and there is cooperation and collaboration. But equally often, conflict results in the kind of competitiveness I have already described, which is not the less fierce for being described in pious clichés as "a matter for prayer."
>
> So the operation gets bigger. If smaller groups get crowded out, maybe that proves that God has lost interest in them. They should have had more "faith." Just as in laissez faire capitalism so in the Christianizing industry . . . survival of the fittest must be the law of God himself.
>
> Obviously some Christian groups feel the pinch more than others. Some denominational missions have large reserves of capital. Wherever the pinch is felt most keenly, there the battle rages most fiercely. And a battle it is. Behind the firm handshakes and ecclesiastical jocularity, a struggle for economic survival often rages, nonetheless deadly for being covert.[4]

The modern thinking about colleges, for example, suggests that not all will survive, except the strongest, the obvious inference being that the weak will perish. Many denominational church groups regularly assess which are their strong and weak churches and what should be done to keep strong churches strong and to help the weak. Not too many denominational leaders would express sadness at the loss of another denomination just as not many pastors would lament the fact that more people come to "my" church and less to "yours." There is no shared commitment on the part of Christian organizations to see that each survives and thrives. Rather, the commitment is to see "my entity grow, at your expense if necessary," and to become as large as possible. If yours doesn't survive, maybe it didn't deserve to continue.

Many church leaders use as their motivation for growth and expansion the salvation of new converts. But as many church groups have learned, it doesn't follow that "new conversions" will always translate into new members. Church growth and efforts at evangelism are not necessarily directly related.

Another central feature of Darwin's theory of evolution was the ongoing improvement that was inherent in the process. This concurred with the "Victorian propensity to believe in progress."[5] As Rifkin observes, however, "the idea of 'no limit' to the process of improvement was not limited to Darwin." He quotes French aristocrat Marquis de Condorcet: "No bounds have been fixed to the improvement of human faculties . . . the perfectability of man is absolutely indefinite. . . ."[6] As Darwin saw it, survival of the fittest was the key point to this ongoing improvement or growth: "[There is] . . . one general law, leading to the advancement of all organic beings, namely, multiply, vary, let the strongest live and the weakest die."[7] Darwin observed that "too many organisms" were "competing for too few niches in nature." He went on to observe that "there are only two ways to promote an organism's survival; either compete for the existing . . . niches or find new ones that have yet to be filled."[8]

One can readily notice the incredible similarities between how organizations, including Christian ones, reflect these Darwinian principles, including use of the latest marketing techniques. One could almost substitute the word *organization* for Darwin's word *organism* and the practical realities would be the same. His suggested way for survival would closely parallel the classic advice in marketing—find a need and fill it. Competition abounds, and to win, "more" is needed.

My involvement with Christian organizations suggests that social Darwinism is alive and well. I'm not suggesting that such is the case in our Christian college science departments. Rather, I'm suggesting that such is the case in terms of organizational operations, particularly the pursuit of students, church members, and donors. Good students, for example, are prime candidates for attention. Each college wants more. And it doesn't matter how many one already has—one more will do. Well-known Christian colleges go to great lengths to "recruit away" students, especially athletes and musicians, they believe would provide great benefit to them. Institutions throw great resources into the fray, including those prime "spiritual" variables such as image, endowment, and library collections. Why? Why do Christian colleges follow the best principles of Darwinism in their efforts to recruit students or raise money? Is survival what life is all about? Can this method be condoned by Scripture?

The irony of this "survival of the fittest" competition is that in terms of their religion, not many Christian colleges or other Christian organizations would identify themselves as supporters of Charles Darwin. But, in their operational practices, Darwin has become one of their best-followed prophets.

Fortunately, Scripture *does* have something to say about all this. It appears that biblical thinking proceeds along two distinct lines. In terms of the intangibles of the kingdom, enough is never enough. But in terms of tangibles, be on your guard because "enough" might be too much. Let me elaborate.

ENOUGH IS NEVER ENOUGH

When I use the term *intangibles* I have in mind concepts like spiritual growth and the fruit of the Spirit. In these matters, Scripture seems to tell us that "enough is never enough." Peter tells us to grow in grace: "But grow in the grace and knowledge of our Lord and Savior Jesus Christ. To him be glory both now and forever! Amen" (2 Peter 3:18). It was said of our Lord: "And Jesus grew in wisdom and stature, and in favor with God and men" (Luke 2:52). Perhaps one of the best illustrations comes from the pen of the Apostle Paul.

In his letter to the Philippians, Paul must have either antici-pated the issue or had been confronted with it—how much is enough? Apparently, there were those in that assembly who were feeling comfortable with their spirituality, who were content to rest on their spiritual laurels. In Philippians 3:12-16, we read Paul's response:

> Not that I have already obtained all this, or have already been made perfect, but I press on to take hold of that for which Christ Jesus took hold of me. Brothers, I do not consider myself yet to have taken hold of it. But one thing I do: Forgetting what is behind and straining toward what is ahead, I press on toward the goal to win the prize for which God has called me heavenward in Christ Jesus.
> All of us who are mature should take such a view of things. And if on some point you think differently, that too God will make clear to you. Only let us live up to what we have already attained.

Among other things, Paul suggests that we do not have the option to look back at our spiritual curriculum vitae and say that enough is enough. Indeed, Paul says that we are to forget all of that and to continue to strive "toward what is ahead" in order "to win the prize" for which God had called him and, presumably, for which God has called us. And then to press home his point, he concludes by saying that his view of this issue is the "mature" one—that those who were mature in the faith would press forward as had he.

In short, when striving for spiritual goals, enough is never enough and our pursuit of them ought always be a very high priority for all Christians, including leaders. Perhaps this issue is the easiest of the two. But, what about tangibles, like money and material possessions?

ENOUGH IS ENOUGH

My reading of Scripture does not suggest precise quantifiable limits that could be interpreted to mean any accumulation beyond a certain number of dollars, members, or buildings is sin and will produce problems. Alternatively, the Bible *does* outline a number of principles which give guidance on the matter of possessions and it's to their delineation that we now turn.

1. *God wants people, and presumably organizations, to accumulate or to de-accumulate only at His command so that hope and trust will always be in Him.* In Joshua 11 there was a huge army "as numerous as the sand on the seashore" being assembled to fend off the vastly outnumbered yet invading Israelites (v. 4). After telling the people that He would give them victory, God told them to make sure to "hamstring their [the enemy's] horses and burn their chariots" (v. 6). Why? Would not the collection of these marvelous instruments of war have done much to aid the Israelites in their next encounter? Yes, but God wanted the people unequivocally to have their dependence on and hope in Him alone. He knew that we humans tend to rely on our tangibles instead of Him. As Yoder has observed, "If . . . we forsake our goods to follow him, we are proclaiming our trust in a Father who knows our needs."[9]

In Joshua 6–8 we see the same principle, but expressed differently. Just before the fall of Jericho, God instructed the people to "keep away from the devoted things" (6:18). Achan failed to obey this command, and he and his family paid with their lives. Later, after the conquest of Ai, the Lord reversed His instructions to the people: "You may carry off their plunder and livestock for yourselves" (8:2). The point is clear: de-accumulation or accumulation was to take place only at His command.

At least three times in the Book of Deuteronomy the people are cautioned about the problems associated with accumulation. Note two of them:

> When the Lord your God brings you into the land he swore to your fathers, to Abraham, Isaac and Jacob, to give you—a land with large, flourishing cities you did not build, houses filled with all kinds of good things you did not provide, wells you did not dig, and vineyards and olive groves you did not plant—then when you eat and are satisfied, be careful that you do not forget the Lord, who brought you out of Egypt, out of the land of slavery (Deuteronomy 6:10-12).

> When you have eaten and are satisfied, praise the Lord your God for the good land he has given you. Be careful that you do not forget the Lord your God. . . . Otherwise, when you

> eat and are satisfied, when you build fine houses and settle down, and when your herds and flocks grow large and your silver and gold increase and all you have is multiplied, then your heart will become proud and you will forget the Lord your God (Deuteronomy 8:10-14).

Examples elsewhere in Scripture could also be cited, but the point seems clear. Excessive accumulation leads to movement away from trust in God. Therefore, accumulation of things ought to take place only with a green light from the Lord. Accumulation ought not always be assumed. Trust in God and obedience to Him—not accumulation—should be our highest priorities. This leads to a second obvious observation.

2. *There comes a point in the accumulation of things where we trust in them and forget about God.* A case in point is God's prediction that the Israelites would reject Him in part because they would come to rely on the bounty of the Promised Land:

> When I have brought them into the land flowing with milk and honey, the land I promised on oath to their forefathers, and when they eat their fill and thrive, they will turn to other gods and worship them, rejecting me and breaking my covenant (Deuteronomy 31:20).

This point is made again in the Minor Prophets: "When I fed them, they were satisfied; when they were satisfied, they became proud; then they forgot me" (Hosea 13:6).

The concept seems clear: there comes a point when accumulation of things and experiencing "success" resulting from that accumulation turns peoples' hearts away from God.

A key inquiry for the leader in this regard would be to answer this question—if our financial strength, if our endowment vanished tomorrow, would I continue to place my trust in God? From His perspective, He wants that trust regardless of our financial resources.

In many ways, one of the reasons we accumulate tangibles is to protect us from the unknown. As Cheryl Forbes observes: "Our insurance industry, our pension systems, our social security program are all designed to protect us—to give us power over the unknown."[10] To the leader of the Christian organization this is one of the goals of an endowment fund. This self-sufficiency or security, however, if taken to an extreme, can serve as a substitute for God. Jeremy Rifkin makes this interesting point:

> God has always been associated with the idea of total self-containment. To be God is to be without need, to be totally self-sufficient and invulnerable.[11]

While one might quarrel with Rifkin's theology, it's not terribly far from God's concern as stated in Deuteronomy and Hosea—"when you become sufficient and content, you forget about Me."

3. *Contentment, for the people of God, is not to be based on the accumulation of things.* As Christian leaders, we can put ourselves in a position of contentment because God says in His Word that He will never forsake us. We are to be content with what we have, whatever it is, and to keep clear of the problems associated with the love of money. Implicit in the concept of contentment is not that we need to de-accumulate—indeed He says be content—but rather if we love what we have, then we need to de-accumulate. This, it seems, was the problem with the rich young ruler—he was not prepared to de-accumulate. He wanted his money to be between him and his love for Jesus, and Jesus in essence said, "It doesn't work that way."

In several different passages, Paul gives us a similar message: don't set your goal on accumulating, but be content with what you have. He tells Timothy:

> But godliness with contentment is great gain. For we brought nothing into the world, and we can take nothing out of it. But if we have food and clothing, we will be content with that. People who want to get rich fall into temptation and a trap and into many foolish and harmful desires that plunge men into ruin and destruction. For the love of money is a root of all kinds of evil. Some people, eager for money, have wandered from the faith and pierced themselves with many griefs (1 Timothy 6:6-10).

Later in that same chapter he instructs Timothy:

> Command those who are rich in this present world not to be

arrogant nor to put their hope in wealth, which is so uncertain, but to put their hope in God, who richly provides us with everything for our enjoyment. Command them to do good, to be rich in good deeds, and to be generous and willing to share. In this way they will lay up treasure for themselves as a firm foundation for the coming age, so that they may take hold of the life that is truly life (vv. 17-19).

Here the instruction for prosperous believers is to de-accumulate so that they may "lay up treasure for themselves . . . for the coming age." Interestingly, one of Paul's descriptions of the godless age to come was that people would be "lovers of money" (2 Timothy 3:2).

Regarding contentment, Paul writes to the Philippians:

I have learned to be content whatever the circumstances. I know what it is to be in need, and I know what it is to have plenty. I have learned the secret of being content in any and every situation, whether well fed or hungry, whether living in plenty or in want. I can do everything through him who gives me strength (Philippians 4:11-13).

Here his emphasis is not necessarily to insist on de-accumulation. Rather, Paul says he knows how to enjoy much or a little because neither money nor circumstances is the source of his contentment—Christ is.

4. *Various Scriptures illustrate the principle that "enough is enough."* Numbers 26, for example, recounts the census of each of the tribes of Israel. Then in verses 53-54, we read:

The land is to be allotted to them as an inheritance based on the number of names. To a larger group give a larger inheritance, and to a smaller group a smaller one; each is to receive its inheritance according to the number of those listed.

Each tribe was not to get the same amount of land in terms of geographical size. Rather, each tribe was given land based on the number of names in each tribe. This suggests limits as to the amount of inheritance each tribe would be given. It was a way of saying enough would be enough. This point is reemphasized in Numbers 27:1-8 and in Numbers 36.

In Numbers 27, the daughters of Zelophehad appealed to Moses for land. They argued that their father died sonless, and since land was assigned to families based on sonship, their family as part of the tribe of Manasseh would not be getting all they were entitled to. When Moses appealed to God, God agreed with the daughters' request (vv. 7-11). Here, the concern seems to be that each tribe receive its rightful inheritance—no more or no less.

Then in Numbers 36:7-9, we read:

> No inheritance in Israel is to pass from tribe to tribe, for every Israelite shall keep the tribal land inherited from his forefathers. Every daughter who inherits land in any Israelite tribe must marry someone in her father's tribal clan, so that every Israelite will possess the inheritance of his fathers. No inheritance may pass from tribe to tribe, for each Israelite tribe is to keep the land it inherits.

The instruction, then, is clear: one tribe's inheritance was not to grow at the expense of another tribe. Wheeling and dealing for a larger share of the "market" was clearly not permitted by God.

Another illustration appears in Leviticus, where instructions were given to the people regarding how to harvest their crops:

> The Lord said to Moses, "Speak to the Israelites and say to them: 'When you enter the land I am going to give you and you reap its harvest, bring to the priest a sheaf of the first grain you harvest' " (Leviticus 23:9-10).

Clearly, the people were not to get all they could from their harvest. Enough was enough. Further, in Leviticus 25, we see God's instructions concerning the sabbatical year, to be celebrated every seventh year in Israel. Amidst the instructions, God asked the question the people most assuredly would be wondering: "You may ask, 'What will we eat in the seventh year if we do not plant or harvest our crops?" (v. 20) Then He answered His own question with an "enough will be enough" reply:

> I will send you such a blessing in the sixth year that the land

will yield enough for three years. While you plant during the eighth year, you will eat from the old crop and will continue to eat from it until the harvest of the ninth year comes in (vv. 21-22).

Ironically, in many Christian circles we have reversed our emphasis of accumulation and de-accumulation. We have placed more organizational effort on the accumulation of tangibles—something which Scripture clearly cautions us about, and we have placed not nearly enough emphasis on the pursuit of intangibles—something the Scriptures strongly encourage us to do.

As Yoder has observed, "Indeed, one of the most frequent and most concrete meanings of the phrase 'God has blessed' in American pious usage is to double the sources of a church agency in increasing in income."[12] If we measure God's blessing by material prosperity, then He has substantially blessed Harvard, Yale, Princeton, and Stanford. As Colson asks, "Is our new property proof of our success? No, I believe that line of thinking is one of the sad delusions of the church. . . . The success of . . . ministry is to be measured not by the size or beauty of its buildings, but by the holy things which happen within them."[13] Note further the cautions of E.M. Bounds:

> No amount of money, genius, or culture can move things for God.[14]

> An increase of educational facilities and a great increase of money force will be the direct curse to religion if they are not sanctified by more and better praying than we are doing.[15]

> The campaign for the twentieth or thirtieth century fund will not help our praying but hinder if we are not careful. Nothing but a specific effort from a praying leadership will avail.[16]

In brief, we have both reversed what appear to be fairly clear biblical priorities and mislabeled them. Why?

First, Christian organizations tend to reward their leaders more for accumulating tangibles than for qualitative growth regarding intangibles. For example, I know of few leaders of Christian liberal arts colleges who were asked to resign because of not enough time spent in prayer. To be sure, there have been those isolated cases where dismissal has resulted because of sexual, financial, or marital indiscretions. Alternatively, I know of a number of leaders who lost their jobs because they were not good enough accumulators—whether of students, money, facilities, or endowment.

Is it not possible that God might want an organization to remain small and possess little in terms of facilities or financial resources? Certainly these comments are not intended to condone mismanagement. From earlier discussions we saw where God had specifically instructed the Israelites not to accumulate and, further, not to take advantage of the latest technology to advance His purposes. Was He wrong and are we right? One would think so given the operating agenda for many Christian organizations.

Leaders of Christian organizations are alert to the ways the game is played. They proceed headily along the road to accumulation of things for their organizations. At a college, for instance, enrollment had better increase, the endowment grow, and buildings be built. It's nice to know that qualitatively students are spending more time praying, that they're living out the commands of Scripture by attending to the needs of the elderly—but that won't lead to a raise or recognition elsewhere, let alone bring one attention for the leadership of the "elite" Christian organizations. By having these kinds of tangible expectations for the leader, corporate boards, by default, implicitly approve operating principles that focus on accumulation.

In my many discussions with pastors of various denominations, they are quick to point out in confidence that their chances for promotion and recognition within their denomination depend on the opportunity to lead the right church. As a result, and without "praying" about it, decisions are made to avoid "serving" in smaller churches in order to optimize their chances for promotion within the denomination. All this is done with the effective use of spiritual-sounding language—"God hasn't led me" or "God has led me to the larger church." Indeed, God could have led that way, but many times our answers as to why we serve where we do amount to nothing more than self-centered, spiritualized lying. Denominational officials play the game in reverse, giving key assignments to pastors who have played the game well in smaller churches. Obviously, one of the significant ways to get the attention of denominational officials is to have rapid church growth and a major, successful building program. Why? Because accumulation of tangibles gets rewarded.

While some boards and church leaders may be at fault for having misplaced priorities in these areas, the leader bent on integrity—whether a college president, pastor, or other organizational official—must accept responsibility for his or her own attitudes and actions. First, a leader has the responsibility to keep priorities and goals biblically based and Christ-centered, regardless of career impact. If one's leadership goal is to make a lot of money and head a prestigious Christian organization, then perhaps another agenda might be warranted. My commitment to Christ ought to say that I will follow Him anytime, anywhere He leads. If He leads to the small, out-of-the-way church, that's OK because He's God, He's promised to meet my *needs*, and I've promised to be obedient. If He takes me to the jungles of a foreign country, that's OK, because He's promised to meet my needs, and I've promised to be obedient. If he leads me to be president of a small, less famous Christian liberal arts college, that's OK too. My sufficiency, after all, does not rest in the tangible assets of the organization I lead, but, rather, in Christ, and in Him alone.

It grieves my heart to hear leaders of Christian organizations talking about how they wouldn't want to go to a particular Christian college or other organization "because of all the problems there." But that's the very point—God is enough! He is the miracle-working God who can take an impossible situation and make it work. We, however, have to give Him the chance to work, and perhaps He wants us to be a part of the solution. One of the most disappointing things for me in the Christian circles I frequent is the way small churches and small Christian organizations including colleges are written off as places where the "biggies" don't want to serve. In the smaller organization, however, there's just as great if not a greater opportunity for leadership skills to be used. Indeed, the problem-laden small organization may require greater leadership skill than the larger, "better-off" one.

The second reason I assign some blame to the leader for this misplaced emphasis on tangible priorities is that leaders have as one of their responsibilities the education of their board. Boards of directors need to be challenged with an organizational commitment to walk by faith just as do individuals.

CONCLUSION AND APPLICATIONS

It is time to wrap up. How much *is* really enough? What kinds of goals should a leader have in this regard? As we have examined, Scripture sets no absolute quantitative guideline in terms of tangibles. Alternatively, Scripture cautions about the problems of over-accumulation and alerts leaders to be sensitive to them. Sadly, too many Christian organizations ignore this issue entirely. It must be addressed. Even though Rifkin's comments are in the context of concerns for biotechnology, they are appropriate here as well:

> This does not mean that our lives should barely be lives; that the best course of action is virtual inaction so as not to use any more of the resources than absolutely necessary to merely survive. *It does mean that we need to continually ask ourselves how much is enough,* and be willing to discipline our appetites so that they remain within the bounds dictated by a sense of fair regard for every other living thing (italics added).[17]

Not only must we keep this question squarely in front of us, but we also need to continually ask how the accumulation of tangibles will impact kingdom needs and priorities.

A few final recommendations. First, *organizations ought to be generous with whatever tangibles have been accumulated.* For instance, many churches might make much better use of underused facilities. Often churches hesitate to allow other groups to use their facilities because "it would bring in the wrong kind of people," itself an incredible irony, or because they don't want the property damaged or harmed (in which case they couch their institutional selfishness in the language of "stewardship for the property the Lord has entrusted to us"). Colleges could also make facilities available at little or no charge for selected groups.

A more radical suggestion, but one that has precedent in Scripture is to tithe organizational income received, whether gift income or endowment income. This is probably already being done by most churches, but why shouldn't Christian colleges or other Christian organizations do likewise? The most prominent arguments raised in opposition to this principle are that "we ought not be giving away 'gift money' that has been given to us as gifts"; and second, "most of our budgets are too low now, and if we gave dollars away, we'd be in even worse shape." Let me respond to the second argument first.

The reason we are commanded to tithe throughout Scripture is not because that by so doing, our economic situation will improve (notwithstanding reflections of some TV preachers to the contrary), but rather because God commands it to illustrate He deserves first place in our lives. Individuals are expected to tithe; why not Christian organizations? Unfortunately, many commands of Scripture seem to become less than practical when applied in an organizational context. Yet God's dealings in the Old Testament were with the Israelites as a corporate entity as much as they were with individuals.

Some colleges, for example, might legitimately argue that they are in essence tithing already because they give gifts to needy students in the form of college-funded student financial aid. This reason has some merit, though usually it's not conceptualized as such on campus. Colleges might also tithe their endowment income. In this way, a college would be expressing its commitment to the greater body of Christ, and perhaps support some alumni ministries along the way.

Back to the first argument, regarding giving away "gift" money; this was precisely the kind of situation faced by the Levites in Numbers 18. Because the Lord was the Levites' inheritance, they were not given any territory in the Promised Land as were the other tribes. God reminded them of this several times. Note, for example, verses 21 and 24:

> I give to the Levites all the tithes in Israel as their inheritance in return for the work they do while serving at the Tent of Meeting. . . . I give to the Levites as their inheritance the tithes that the Israelites present as an offering to the Lord. That is why I said concerning them: "They will have no inheritance among the Israelites."

The Levites received tithes or gifts from the people. But the fact that they were priests, the fact that they lived off of the gifts of others, did not excuse them from their responsibility to tithe as well. Note also verses 25-26, 28:

The Lord said to Moses, "Speak to the Levites and say to them: 'When you receive from the Israelites the tithe I give you as your inheritance, you must present a tenth of that tithe as the Lord's offering. . . . In this way you also will present an offering to the Lord from all the tithes you receive from the Israelites. From these tithes you must give the Lord's portion to Aaron the priest.' "

What would be the impact on the kingdom if the ten largest Christian organizations, in terms of endowment, would redistribute 10 percent of their earnings to other Christian organizations, or even to the struggling Christian colleges?

A second recommendation: *organizations need to de-accumulate.* Most organizations have excess or unneeded books (from library weeding or bookstore inventory), related supplies, and unneeded and outdated equipment that could be effectively used elsewhere in the kingdom. Some organizations might even want to consider the concept of a loaned executive or faculty member, thus allowing a struggling organization to temporarily benefit from the personal services of one of their valuable employees. Many Christian organizations, including churches, need to abandon plans to accumulate endowment funds. It is my belief that only those organizations which charge for their services ought to pursue endowment funds. And a word of advice to those who do. Such organizations are in essence saying they're not "faith-only" operations and, therefore, ought not delude themselves into saying, "We're an organization that depends solely on God to meet our needs." The truth is more likely to be that the organization expects the consumer or user of services to do the trusting in God to meet needs.

Finally, *leaders ought to focus on making even more significant investments in spiritual growth both in themselves and the people who work for them.* People need to be encouraged to "seek first His kingdom." Bounds points in this same direction when he states:

> The plea and purpose of the apostles were to put the church to praying. They did not ignore the grace of cheerful giving. They were not ignorant of the place which religious activity and work occupied in the spiritual life; but not one nor all of

them, in apostolic estimate or urging, could at all compare in necessity and importance with prayer.[18]

This distinctive *must* characterize our churches and our Christian organizations, and it is the function of leaders to constantly model it. We must become known more for our intangible priorities than for our beautiful buildings and large enrollments and endowments. We have to be more than Christian clubs.

In a recent report on the University of Chicago, president Hanna Gray observed that the financial state of the university "may be summarized by the words of the lady who said, 'I have enough money to last me the rest of my life, unless I buy something.' " God's love constrains us to be in the business of accumulating intangibles, not buying tangibles. Christian churches and organizations will probably not move in this direction unless they are led by men and women of God who regularly and seriously address the question, "How much is enough?"

Then Moses gave an order and they sent this word throughout the camp: "No man or woman is to make anything else as an offering for the sanctuary." And so the people were restrained from bringing more, because what they already had was more than enough to do all the work (Exodus 36: 6-7).

LEADERSHIP—THE PERSONAL DIMENSION

This chapter will discuss the personal dimension of leadership by dividing it into four major categories: the spiritual, the physical, the family, and the intellectual. Each are crucial factors in making the leader all he or she can be for the Lord.

THE SPIRITUAL DIMENSION

Some argue that whenever the spiritual dimension of a problem or issue is discussed, the danger exists of separating it from other important considerations (i.e., nonspiritual dimensions). By highlighting a spiritual dimension to leadership, however, I am not intending to create a sacred/secular dichotomy. I too believe that the spiritual dimension cuts across all of life. I highlight the spiritual dimension in order to give it increased emphasis, knowing full well that the spiritual part of me impacts all the rest.

Without question, effectiveness in leadership requires meaningful progress along the path to spiritual maturity. It involves the process of constantly giving as much of myself as I know to as much of Christ as I know. As I daily discover more and more who I am, and as I constantly learn more about His love for me, I strive to press on toward becoming what He desires for me. He tells me that if I desire to be a leader, I desire a noble task but that leadership requires the following qualities:

Now the overseer must be above reproach, the husband of

but one wife, temperate, self-controlled, respectable, hospitable, able to teach, not given to much wine, not violent but gentle, not quarrelsome, not a lover of money. He must manage his own family well and see that his children obey him with proper respect. (If anyone does not know how to manage his own family, how can he take care of God's church?) He must not be a recent convert, or he may become conceited and fall under the same judgment as the devil. He must also have a good reputation with outsiders, so that he will not fall into disgrace and into the devil's trap (1 Timothy 3:2-7).

Scripture teaches that, as I desire to follow after Christ, whether as leader or follower, my life is to reflect the qualities set forth in 2 Peter 1:5-8—faith, goodness, knowledge, self-control, perseverance, godliness, brotherly kindness, and love. The Scripture furthermore enjoins me, through the power of God's Spirit, to reflect in my life the fruit of the Spirit: "But the fruit of the Spirit is love, joy, peace, patience, kindness, goodness, faithfulness, gentleness and self-control. Against such things there is no law" (Galatians 5:22-23). As one who desires to be mature in my lifestyle, I'm exhorted to reflect the qualities of discernment:

Anyone who lives on milk, being still an infant, is not acquainted with the teaching about righteousness. But solid food is for the mature, who by constant use have trained themselves to distinguish good from evil (Hebrews 5:13-14).

And there are a variety of other instructions regarding discipleship.

One of the most useful sets of instructions for leaders, in my opinion, is the following Old Testament passage:

After the death of Moses the servant of the Lord, the Lord said to Joshua son of Nun, Moses' aide: "Moses my servant is dead. Now then, you and all these people, get ready to cross the Jordan River into the land I am about to give to them—to the Israelites. I will give you every place where you set your foot, as I promised Moses. Your territory will extend from the desert and from Lebanon to the great river, the Euphrates—all the Hittite country—and to the Great Sea on the west. No one will be able to stand up against you all the days of your life. As I was with Moses, so I will be with you; I will never leave you or forsake you.

"Be strong and courageous, because you will lead these people to inherit the land I swore to their forefathers to give them. Be strong and very courageous. Be careful to obey all the law my servant Moses gave you; do not turn from it to the right or to the left, that you may be successful wherever you go. Do not let this Book of the Law depart from your mouth; meditate on it day and night, so that you may be careful to do everything written in it. Then you will be prosperous and successful. Have I not commanded you?" (Joshua 1:1-9)

As the baton was passed from Moses to Joshua, God gave His newly chosen leader guidelines for successful leadership. I'd like to highlight several of them.

First, *God had Joshua's attention,* for He was able to speak to him. I can look back on times in my leadership when God couldn't speak to me because I failed to place myself in a position where I could listen to Him. Thus, an important requisite for leadership is that we regularly put ourselves in a position to hear His voice. In other words, the lines of communication must be kept open through Bible reading, meditation, and prayer.

Second, *God gave Joshua a goal to achieve.* Many times in leadership roles man devises his goals and then he asks God to bless them. As leaders we must become more conscious of making sure His goals are our goals. God has given us such promises as:

I will instruct you and teach you in the way you should go; I will counsel you and watch over you (Psalm 32:8).

This is what the Lord says—your Redeemer, the Holy One of Israel: "I am the Lord your God, who teaches you what is best for you, who directs you in the way you should go" (Isaiah 48:17).

What's more, He cautions us about following plans that are not His:

"Woe to the obstinate children," declares the Lord, "to those who carry out plans that are not mine, forming an alliance, but not by my Spirit, heaping sin upon sin; who go down to Egypt without consulting me; who look for help to Pharaoh's protection, to Egypt's shade for refuge" (Isaiah 30:1-2).

Third, *God's plan for Joshua required action on Joshua's part.* The Lord told Joshua that he would be given every place where he set his foot. In short, the scope of his achievement would depend on the extent of his action. Many times we do nothing, expecting God to do all the work. Of course, sometimes that is exactly the thing to do—nothing—and watch God give the victory. Other times, however, God wants us to be co-laborers with Him to complete a task. Most leaders have known those times when little is expected from God and He honors our expectations! Other times, I believe, He's prepared to do far more than we expect. We need to pray like Jabez:

Jabez cried out to the God of Israel, "Oh, that you would bless me and enlarge my territory! Let your hand be with me, and keep me from harm so that I will be free from pain." And God granted his request (1 Chronicles 4:10).

Fourth, *God promised Joshua success even before Joshua started; further, He promised Joshua His abiding presence.* Think of it! Even before Joshua began the task, he was assured victory. Some may think it presumptuous to believe that God will always give victory over a foe, as was the case here. Perhaps. The problem many times is that the plan we're pursuing is not His but ours. And yes, God never promises the price will be cheap (cf. Hebrews 11:35-40). However, if we hear His voice, if the plans are His, and if He has promised success, then we need to pray for enlarged boundaries.

Fifth, *Joshua was to be completely obedient to the law of God.* "Do not turn from it to the right or to the left," the Lord commanded (Joshua 1:7). Leaders constantly face the issue of incomplete obedience. The leader or the people being led sometimes want to be only partially biblical. As I tell our students, in being biblical we must be biblical. In other words, we must not settle for pursuing biblical ends using unbiblical methods. This is one of the concerns, for example, addressed in Larry Richards' book, *The Screw-loose Letters*.[1] We can only imagine the results that incomplete obedience would have produced in the following biblical contexts: Noah builds a smaller ark? Joshua marches around Jericho *three* times? Gideon uses 30,000 troops?

Sixth, *Joshua was to be preoccupied with the Word of God*, day and night. As noted earlier, not enough Christian leaders are preoccupied with God's Word. And when boards reward leaders more on quantitative performance (more members, more students, more buildings, more funds raised) than for qualitative performance, they may be contributing to the demise both of the leader and the organization.

While other observations could be made, I want to reiterate the fact that *qualitative spiritual development is indispensable to effective leadership.*

THE PHYSICAL DIMENSION

DIET/REST/EXERCISE. My observation tells me that these are not only concerns personally ("Oh, what's so bad about carrying around an extra ten to fifteen pounds?" we rationalize), but the conservative Christian culture tells me that slippage in this area is not quite so bad as slippage in other areas. Let me explain.

I grew up in a conservative church which quite often had visiting evangelists. The basic thrust of their sermons was something to this effect—don't drink, don't smoke, don't dance, save others, witness, and prepare for heaven. I never heard any sermons pertaining to the care of my body, the dangers of overeating, and the importance of diet and exercise. One of the strongest advocates of the "don't drink or smoke" line was a 300-plus-pound evangelist. It didn't dawn on me until later in life that the issue for the believer is stewardship of one's body, whether the problem is food abuse, drug abuse (e.g., pills, alcohol, coffee), improper rest, or lack of exercise. As Paul reminds us in 1 Corinthians 3:16-17, the body is God's temple:

> Don't you know that you yourselves are God's temple and that God's Spirit lives in you? If anyone destroys God's temple, God will destroy him; for God's temple is sacred, and you are that temple.

179

As a result of my background, it is always easier for me to tolerate persons with weight problems than those with alcohol problems. Sadly, many in Christian organizations are substantially overweight.

Given the frequent and seemingly never-ending schedule of dinners, banquets, and homemade pies and cookies that must be sampled, it's very easy for the leader to struggle in this area. Yet proper diet, rest, and exercise are critically essential for the leader. While short-term neglect in these areas will not immediately produce negative results, long-term neglect may prove disastrous.

Oswald Sanders tells the following story of Robert Murray McCheyne: "When . . . McCheyne was dying at the age of thirty-two—he had overspent himself in revival work and so forth—he told a friend at his bedside, 'God gave me a horse to ride and a message to deliver. Alas, I have killed the horse and I can't deliver the message.'" Sanders concludes, "I am not suggesting for a moment that you become oversolicitous for yourself or care for yourself too much or be afraid to spend. But there's a point when it is wise to stop and have a rest."[2]

Rules I try to follow include the following: (1) get adequate rest (for me at least seven hours); (2) seldom eat breads; (3) eat only several bites of desserts; and (4) participate in exercise that does not require a specified playing area. For example, I enjoy basketball, but when I travel, it's hard to find a gym. Jogging, then, is a much better alternative for me, as I can usually find a street! For those who do little traveling, basketball, swimming, tennis, or racquetball may be good types of regular exercise.

The point I make is simple to state but hard to practice: the proper care of one's body is critically important to the leader. There are enough other stress points in leadership. This ought not be one of them.

SEXUALITY. Divorce and marital infidelity (and the two are not always related) claim an increasing number of evangelical leaders each year. The purpose of this section is not to identify names or to assign blame. All leaders, however, probably have to admit, at least to themselves, that this issue is a troubling one. John Stott has observed, "Nobody (with the sole exception of Jesus of Nazareth) has been sexually sinless. There is no question, therefore, of coming to this study with a horrid 'holier-than-thou' attitude of moral superiority."[3] The article entitled "The War Within: An Anatomy of Lust,"[4] which appeared in *Leadership* magazine several years ago, contains issues that many Christian leaders have at one time or another had to struggle with.

Today's culture, including the Christian one, oozes with the overtones of sexuality, and indeed, it has invaded the executive suite. As Forbes has observed:

> Sexuality is one of the oldest means to power. Kings, and the occasional queen, have used it, as have the common husband and wife. It operates in businesses and schools, wherever people intermingle. Of all the means to power—intellectual, financial, psychological—it is the most basic. Everyone practices it, Christians and non-Christians alike. No matter how much we want to avoid it, we cannot talk about power without talking about sex.[5]

Sexuality is part and parcel of almost all television shows, movies, and songs. The Christian response has typically been to ignore the issue of sexuality. We feel comfortable discussing God's love, but quite uncomfortable discussing the love between man and woman. When was the last time, for example, you heard a Christian song about love and marriage? I must admit, however, that an increasing number of Christian books deal with the subject.

Many Christian organizations, furthermore, are almost totally devoid of women in the executive suite. Only a handful of evangelical Christian colleges have women in senior management positions. Other Christian organizations reflect a similar pattern. Why? Has God distributed His gifts on the basis of sex, after all?

Part of the problem with having women in the executive suite may be in part related to sexuality. Men in the Christian culture have not been used to having to compete with women as peers. What's more, women in the executive suite may create uncomfortable situations when typical professional assignments, such as overnight travel to conventions, are necessary.

Though others are more qualified to write about this subject, I would nevertheless like to make a few observations. First, *leaders must accept and harness their sexuality.* Stott notes:

> We are all sexual beings. Our sexuality, according to both

Scripture and experience, is basic to our humanness. Angels may be sexless; we humans are not. When God made humankind, he made us male and female. So to talk about sex is to touch a point close to the centre of our personality. Our very identity is being discussed, and perhaps either endorsed or threatened. So the subject demands an unusual degree of sensitivity.[6]

We can't deny the way God made us. The sexual drive is a powerful one. Accordingly, the leader who takes the attitude, "I never have to worry about that," is quickly going to find himself or herself in trouble. Indeed, the intensity of this normal part of who we are should prepare us to be on our guard about sexual improprieties.

In my discussions with leaders who have failed in this area, they usually observe that sexual sin is not always premeditated. Further, it doesn't always result from a lack of love or affection for one's spouse. Rather, it results from the frequency of contact and time spent together on the job. As Forbes observes:

Sexual response between men and women is always present and nearly automatic. We need to recognize this, and though we can't dispel it completely, we can avoid deliberately using sexuality for power.[7]

The secular literature, for example, when describing the boss/secretary relationship often refers to the secretary as the "office wife." As Pascale and Athos note, "One's secretary is often one's lone outpost of the personal in an otherwise largely impersonal organizational world."[8] This is not to suggest that the sexual intimacy of the husband/wife relationship is present, but other similarities to the husband/wife relationship certainly may be. The exhortation to the leader then, "Be on your guard," is highly appropriate.

I also want to make it clear that I am not assigning culpability for sexual sin only to the "other women" a leader works with. Obviously, the responsibility to be prudent is both on the leader and on those with whom he works. Many male leaders, for example, tend to place the blame for their sexual downfall on other women: "My wife failed to meet my needs," "I was seduced." Unconsciously, many male leaders hold to the assumption: "If women aren't seducing righteous men of God now, they are at least destroying their sexuality and weakening their wills."[9] As Forbes notes, "The excuse is as old as Adam, and just as morally corrupt now as it was then."[10]

Leaders—both men and women—simply have to say no to sexual temptations. They must remember that God is not in the business of tempting people:

When tempted, no one should say, "God is tempting me." For God cannot be tempted by evil, nor does he tempt anyone; but each one is tempted when, by his own evil desire, he is dragged away and enticed. Then, after desire has conceived, it gives birth to sin; and sin, when it is full-grown, gives birth to death (James 1:13-15).

The models of leaders in Scripture, particularly those in the Old Testament, suggest that the issue of sexuality has been a problem throughout history. David's consummated lust produced tragic consequences for his family and others.

This is what the Lord says: "Out of your household I am going to bring calamity upon you. Before your very eyes I will take your wives and give them to one who is close to you, and he will lie with your wives in broad daylight. You did it in secret, but I will do this thing in broad daylight before all Israel. . . ." But because by doing this you have made the enemies of the Lord show utter contempt, the son born to you will die (2 Samuel 12:11-12,14).

Solomon's preoccupation with sex and women led to his downfall:

King Solomon, however, loved many foreign women besides Pharaoh's daughter—Moabites, Ammonites, Edomites, Sidonians and Hittites. . . . He had seven hundred wives of royal birth and three hundred concubines, and his wives led him astray. As Solomon grew old, his wives turned his heart after other gods, and his heart was not fully devoted to the Lord his God (1 Kings 11:1-4).

There are other examples of leaders in the Bible who played "fast and loose" in the area of sexuality. No wonder the repeated warnings in Proverbs:

> It [wisdom] will save you also from the adulteress, from the wayward wife with her seductive words, who has left the partner of her youth and ignored the covenant she made before God. For her house leads down to death. . . . None who go to her return (Proverbs 2:16-19).

> For the lips of an adulteress drip honey, and her speech is smoother than oil; but in the end she is bitter as gall, sharp as a double-edged sword. Her feet go down to death; her steps lead straight to the grave. She gives no thought to the way of life; her paths are crooked, but she knows it not. Now then, my sons, listen to me; do not turn aside from what I say. Keep to a path far from her, do not go near the door of her house, lest you give your best strength to others (Proverbs 5:3-9).

> Drink water from your own cistern, running water from your own well. Should your springs overflow in the streets, your streams of water in the public squares? Led them be yours alone, never to be shared with strangers. May your fountain be blessed, and may you rejoice in the wife of your youth. A loving doe, a graceful deer—may her breasts satisfy you always, may you ever be captivated by her love. Why be captivated, my son, by an adulteress? Why embrace the bosom of another man's wife? (Proverbs 5:15-20)

The point, again, is for the leader to be ever alert in this area. No leader is immune from temptations; therefore, he or she must always be prepared with a biblical response. Some leaders handle other kinds of temptations very well; they struggle, however, when dealing with sexual temptation. Perhaps as Paul prayed for deliverance from his "thorn in the flesh," deliverance from lust can likewise be sought. The words of Paul in response to his unanswered prayer are still alive with power:

> Three times I pleaded with the Lord to take it away from me. But he said to me, "My grace is sufficient for you, for my

power is made perfect in weakness." Therefore I will boast all the more gladly about my weaknesses, so that Christ's power may rest on me. That is why, for Christ's sake, I delight in weaknesses, in insults, in hardships, in persecutions, in difficulties. For when I am weak, then I am strong (2 Corinthians 12:8-10).

What are some practical guidelines that might help combat sexual temptation? First, since the eyes and the mind are critically involved with lust, leaders ought to avoid "stopping to gaze" at hotel and airport newsstands. Buy the newspaper and run. Second, when in a hotel room, consider not turning on the TV and rely instead on a radio. Too many times I have found myself tempted to watch an HBO movie ("Of course I can handle it!"), so I have learned that the best defense is simply not to watch the TV. Third, always keep your spouse informed of time spent out of the office with a member of the opposite sex, whether lunch, business trip, or otherwise. Your spouse will appreciate your honesty and by so doing you will have achieved a built-in accountability against "secretive" meetings. Fourth, when possible, and when a business trip requires time together away from the office, especially for overnight trips, make sure a third party knows about it, and if possible, make sure another person goes along. The business trip does not always require that "just the two of you" go. Indeed, if you want it to be "just the two of you," perhaps this is an indication that the relationship is already more than just a business one. Richard Foster, in his book *Money, Sex, and Power* gives yet another guideline: "no extramarital genital sex."[11] In a high tech society, "high touch" is a useful concept, but not with regard to genital sex. He further argues that "expression of non-genital sexuality [should] be controlled [for] the good of the marriage and the well-being of the spouse."[12]

Other guidelines could be suggested, but my chief point is this: in order to reflect sexual purity in lifestyle, the leader must be especially alert to and avoid sexual temptation. As Paul admonished us:

The body is not meant for sexual immorality, but for the Lord, and the Lord for the body. . . . Do you not know that he who unites himself with a prostitute is one with her in body? For it is said, "The two will become one flesh." But he who unites himself with the Lord is one with him in spirit.

Flee from sexual immorality. All other sins a man commits are outside his body, but he who sins sexually sins against his own body. Do you not know that your body is a temple of the Holy Spirit, who is in you, whom you have received from God? You are not your own; you were bought at a price. Therefore honor God with your body (1 Corinthians 6:13, 16-20).

THE FAMILY DIMENSION

SPOUSE. "Jim Smith is thirty-eight years old. He has a pretty wife, two beautiful children, and is considered one of the outstanding pastors in his city. Jim and Jane were married while Jim was still in seminary. Their first child was born during his senior year. Jane never completed her college education but took a job to help Jim through seminary. Jim is an effective preacher and is greatly respected by both his assistant pastor and the congregation. He works hard on his sermons. His church is growing. *Jim's wife will leave him next week.*"

"Bob Ramson is the executive director of Christian Commitment Abroad, which he founded twenty-two years ago. He has traveled all over the world and is a much sought-after speaker. After a shaky beginning, CCA began to grow rapidly about ten years ago. Much of its growth is due to Bob's high level of commitment and his willingness to give himself unstintingly to the work of Christ. *Bob doesn't know it, but he left his wife and children eight years ago.*"

These two anecdotes, both from Engstrom and Dayton's book, *The Christian Executive*,[13] aptly illustrate the situations too often faced by Christian leaders—they have failed in their marriages.

Paul's qualifications for overseers and deacons included the requirement that these leaders be the "husband of but one wife" (1 Timothy 3:2). And just what kind of husband did he have in mind? He answers this in Ephesians 5:25-33:

> Husbands, love your wives, just as Christ loved the church and gave himself up for her to make her holy, cleansing her by the washing with water through the word, and to present

her to himself as a radiant church, without stain or wrinkle or any other blemish, but holy and blameless. In this same way, husbands ought to love their wives as their own bodies. He who loves his wife loves himself. After all, no one ever hated his own body, but he feeds and cares for it, just as Christ does the church—for we are members of his body. "For this reason a man will leave his father and mother and be united to his wife, and the two will become one flesh." This is a profound mystery—but I am talking about Christ and the church. However, each of you also must love his wife as he loves himself, and the wife must respect her husband.

Clearly, the husband is to love his wife as Christ loved the church. He ought to love his wife as he loves his own body.

Sadly, many leaders have begun an idolatrous relationship with another mistress—she's called "the ministry." This mistress demands long hours, time away from home, and is used to justify all kinds of unbiblical priorities. This kind of idolatry must be labeled for what it is—sin. The illicit affairs with the corporate mistress have got to stop. God's priorities cannot be ignored. He expects leaders to love their spouses as He loved the church. And this requires that the leader not neglect the needs—all of them—of the spouse. As Engstrom and Dayton note:

> Some of us immediately respond in our own defense, "But this is the ministry to which God has *called* me! My wife understands that. That's one of the sacrifices we are making together." Perhaps. But perhaps that is your view of the situation, and although it may be outwardly shared by your wife, perhaps inwardly . . . she feels quite differently. Too often the Christian wife is put in the position of appearing to oppose the will of the Lord if she does not feel at ease with the circumstance within which her husband is moving. Many men and women marry before they have a clear picture of the ministry to which they (or he) may be called. Too often they overlook what the Spirit may be saying to her and what gifts God may have bestowed upon her.[14]

If this kind of spousal relationship characterizes the life of the leader, we have done an absolutely dismal job of practicing Christlike love. We must start over. Too soon is not soon enough. In terms of family priorities, one's spouse must be made number one and the spouse must know it.

Following are some suggestions that might be considered in regard to developing and strengthening the relationship with one's spouse. First, take regular vacations with *only* your spouse at least several times per year, even if they are only day-long outings. I am amazed and surprised at how many leaders do not spend much time vacationing with their spouses. Vacation times without children are especially important for developing intimacy, both sexual and otherwise. Second, in addition to doing a variety of support activities around the house, do something special for your spouse on a consistent basis. One of the habits suggested to me many years ago was to bring home cut flowers for my wife— every week if possible. I have not succeeded every week, but I hit that goal more often than I miss it. This $10-15 monthly expenditure is one of the best investments I can make in my marriage. Once in a while, slip in something additional, like new clothes or jewelry. Third, spend time with your spouse. The issue of "when" has to be worked out by each couple, but don't let that keep you from finding the time to be together. Fourth, make sure your spouse understands the family financial situation and make sure she is financially cared for in the event of your death. Too many leaders keep their spouses uninformed in these kind of matters. Discuss them openly and forthrightly.

Engstrom and Dayton offer additional suggestions:

> Start asking your wife for dates, just the two of you together. . . . Ask her to evaluate how she sees you spending your time. . . . Try to fantasize what you believe would be the very best situation for you as individuals and as a couple ten years from now.[15]

Don't believe the lie that your spouse will settle for "a little bit of quality time." The spouse appreciates quality time, to be sure, but large doses of quality time is what the spouse deserves. Just as our Heavenly Father desires significant amounts of both quality and quantity time of us, so too do our spouses.

Engstrom and Dayton provide another reminder to leaders:

God's work *will* get done without you. God is really not nervous about the future. Isn't He much more concerned with what you *are* than with what you accomplish, and isn't what you are demonstrated by the relationships you have? And isn't the most profound of those relationships the one you have with your wife? Have you left your wife? We pray she will take you back.[16]

They also have provided the following checklist for leaders to test whether or not they have "left their spouses." If the leader answers yes to most of these statements, perhaps "you've already left your wife or are in the process of leaving her":

How Do You Stand?

( ) I usually take work home at night.
( ) I haven't had a date with my wife in two weeks.
( ) I don't have a date with my wife listed in my appointment book.
( ) I usually work away from home more than ten hours each day.
( ) We have had two fights in the last two weeks.
( ) We haven't had a fight in five years.
( ) I have four or more years education beyond my wife.
( ) We married before I was called to my present task.
( ) Our youngest child is 16 to 20.
( ) My wife hasn't been on a trip with me in four years.
( ) Most of our social relationships revolve around my work.
( ) The family dinner is often interrupted by phone calls for me.
( ) My wife has little understanding of how my organization works.
( ) My wife has had no additional formal education since we were married.
( ) My wife does not have any career plans outside of our marriage.[17]

A concluding thought. Aside from the general observations identified thus far, this area of the spousal relationship is one in which the Bible does not provide many actual examples. In other words, Scripture instructs us how to properly love and care for our spouses, but it doesn't provide many cases of extended dialogue between husband and wife, especially about the kinds of issues which dominate contemporary marriage relationships. While we gain quite a few insights into the wives of Abraham, Job, and Jacob, we know little about the wives of Joseph, Peter, Joshua, and Moses. We don't know for sure just what roles they played in the ministries of their husbands.

Take Moses, for instance. We do know that when God called Moses to return to Egypt from his forty years of shepherding, he returned with his wife and two sons: "So Moses took his wife and sons, put them on a donkey and started back to Egypt. And he took the staff of God in his hand" (Exodus 4:20). But during the exodus, Zipporah and her sons returned to her father in Midian and only occasionally did they visit Moses thereafter (see Exodus 18:2, 5). Why this arrangement? We never are told.

CHILDREN. While donors, deacons, and many others can get the leader's attention with little effort, the leader's children often are not so fortunate. As a general observation, children can survive with minimal attention. And some get precious little from their leader/parent. Alternatively, children will take as much time as they are given.

Let's look first as some biblical observations about the leader's involvement with his children. According to the Old Testament, God clearly expected parents to teach children biblical truths because without it the nation of Israel would not long survive. Note the following references:

> Impress them [God's commandments] on your children. Talk about them when you sit at home and when you walk along the road, when you lie down and when you get up. Tie them as symbols on your hands and bind them on your foreheads. Write them on the doorframes of your houses and on your gates (Deuteronomy 6:7-9).

> Teach them [these words of mine] to your children, talking about them when you sit at home and when you walk along the road, when you lie down and when you get up. Write them on the doorframes of your houses and on your gates, so that your days and the days of your children may be many

in the land that the Lord swore to give your forefathers, as many as the days that the heavens are above the earth (Deuteronomy 11:19-21).

Take to heart all the words I have solemnly declared to you this day, so that you may command your children to obey carefully all the words of this law. They are not just idle words for you—they are your life. By them you will live long in the land you are crossing the Jordan to possess (Deuteronomy 32:46-47).

This concern for children is additionally set forth in Psalm 78:4:

We will not hide them from their children; we will tell the next generation the praiseworthy deeds of the Lord, his power, and the wonders he has done.

In brief, a leader has a responsibility for the biblical education of his family.

Good books which provide input for parents on the subject of rearing children are numerous. The purpose of this discussion is not to duplicate them. Instead, I want to set forth some of the ways the leader might work at this important priority.

First, *leaders might not be able to follow some formalized plan.* What worked with our children when they were preschoolers, for example, doesn't work now. Not only have we changed, but they have also changed and so has our schedule. Much of the schedule change is related to my position as president of a college and to the accelerated number of after-school and weekend activities the kids find themselves involved with. However, we have found that the four teachable moments mentioned in Deuteronomy 6 (when we get up in the morning, at mealtime, when we take trips together, and at bedtime) have remained teachable moments regardless of the children's ages. Teachable moments are not always capable of being scheduled. They present themselves at various times and in various ways. Our goal as parents, therefore, is to be with our children as much as we can (both individually and together) to make the most of these teachable moments.

We have also found that we have had to be flexible. What started out as "family night" when the children were much smaller evolved into "family time" as they became older. In other words, in addition to scheduled times together, we have actively worked at more spontaneous activities as well.

We have discovered a number of practical things which work well for us as a family. *First,* we try to have breakfast out with one of the children each Sunday morning before church. Since we have three children, I take one each for three weeks and then my wife does likewise. We've been doing this for more than ten years. It's been fun for us to see the changes in the nature of conversation. The kids still look forward to that time.

Second, we've taken up some family recreational activities that *all* of us can enjoy together—for example, snow skiing serves us well.

Third, I hardly ever take work home from the office. I mean this in two ways. First, I mean it psychologically. Leaders have to work hard to make sure the problems of the office don't become the problems of the home. Second, I refer to physical work—I don't bring home a briefcase stuffed full of office business. When the children were much smaller, they couldn't understand why Daddy couldn't play when he was home. Somehow, I was unable to translate "I must study" or "I have this report to complete" into "children-ese." As a result, I've changed my habits so that when I'm home from the office I'm available to spend time with my family. There are many nights, however, when I have to return to the office to work late.

Fourth, we repeatedly emphasize the benefits of leadership to our family. Often it's easy to focus on the detriments of being a leader. To be sure there are many. But benefits are also plentiful. Our children, for example, have gotten to meet many interesting people whom we have hosted in our home. They have often traveled with us to speaking engagements, and we have taken side-tours of interest to them. Plus, we've had the additional benefit of uninterrupted "talk" time which travel affords.

Fifth, we have had to recognize that we will carry out leadership responsibilities differently when our children are no longer in our home. This is another way of saying that the leadership agenda is different when the responsibility for young children is involved than when they are not. I'm exceedingly grateful for a supportive board of trustees that lets us live out our family priorities. I would encourage other boards to do likewise.

I share these observations about children knowing full well

that being parents who desire godliness for their children does not necessarily assure godly children. There are frequent Scripture references, for example, where a godly leader was followed by an ungodly son who was followed by a godly son and so on. Just reread 1–2 Kings or 1–2 Chronicles and you'll get the picture! As leader/parents, then, all the Lord asks is that we simply do our best and continually cast our children on Him and His grace.

Finally, I identify with the observation attributed to Thomas Howard—that he would never tell anyone else how to raise children until after he saw his great-grandchildren following after Christ.

THE INTELLECTUAL DIMENSION

Many leaders stop growing intellectually after they achieve given positions of leadership. Degrees are secured and classes are taken primarily to present the proper set of credentials for the job. The leader who fails to aggressively pursue further cognitive development, however, will not long be an effective leader.

While formal classwork is always an option, and I would add, I have always found it to be extremely stimulating, that is not the only option. One of the advantages of formal classwork is that it contains a built-in element of risk. After the degree is secured, it is very tempting to avoid placing oneself in a position again where academic failure can result. "After all, I have enough risks attached to leadership responsibilities. I don't need more." This kind of risk, however, can serve as a catalyst for growth. So from time to time formal coursework ought to be considered. Institutes and workshops may also be useful.

Additionally, the leader ought to be an avid reader, both of works pertinent to leadership and others totally outside of one's given vocation, including those by secular as well as Christian authors. And I'm obviously assuming that this type of reading will not be in lieu of Bible reading and study.

According to Gordon MacDonald, "The development of the mind makes it possible for men and women to be servants to the generations in which they live. . . . We do not develop our intellects merely for our own personal advancement, but we put our thinking power to work for the use of others. . . . As my mind grows, it may make possible the growth of others."[18] And Oswald Sanders observes, "The man who desires to grow spiritually and intellectually will be constantly at his books."[19] Among other reasons for encouraging reading, Sanders notes the following: mental stimulation, cultivation of style, acquisition of information, and fellowship with great minds.[20]

It is also important for the leader to set aside time for what former colleague William Green calls reflective leadership. Much of leadership, at least in the organizational context, involves scheduled meetings, responding to complaints, and the like. Yet if the leader is to lead, time must be spent, repeatedly, away from the office, reflecting on the enterprise. One of the key responsibilities of a board is to make sure the leader takes time for reflective leadership. My period for reflective leadership includes large doses of reading material, which obviously enhances cognitive development. Further, my expectation for each of our senior-level administrators is that they take at least one week per year in addition to vacation time out of the office pursuing this reflective function.

Frequently leaders lose sight of the overall purposes and mission of an organization. Sustained quiet time for reflection outside of the office helps retain perspective in this important responsibility.

CHAPTER
THIRTEEN

LEADERSHIP—THE PROFESSIONAL DIMENSION

In the last chapter, we discussed the personal dimension of leadership. Now we'll tackle the just-as-critical professional dimension, particularly as it refers to compensation, transitions, and vulnerability.

COMPENSATION

Leaders are definitely "worth" the big salaries they are paid. Or at least so goes the thinking of many who consider pursuing a leadership position. While not often verbalized, at least not initially, the issue of "how much will I get paid?" is an important criterion to the potential leader. As the unwritten rules of the hiring process are now set forth, it's not appropriate for the leadership candidate to raise pecuniary issues until at least final interviews take place, or preferably, once an offer is extended. Then and only then should financial discussions take place.

My assertion for the remainder of this discussion is that "leaders chosen by God" should seldom if ever raise concerns, other than perhaps for purposes of clarification, pertaining to the economic issues of their employment. I'll give my reasons later.

Many leaders negotiate or bargain for a "top" salary/ benefits package and only accept "if the price is right." The assumption which underlies this kind of thinking is that the organization should take care of the leader's needs and then the leader will take care of the needs of the organization. And since the pressure

195

of leadership is so great, a large salary, presumably to compensate for this stress, is called for. This attitude seems to be the reverse of that presented in Scripture, which is: if I'm called by God, I have a responsibility to take care of the needs of the people (remember our earlier reference to the leader as a shepherd?) and then God and the people will take care of my needs. If I have negative stress, God tells me to "cast my care on Him," not ask for more money and benefits. The actions of both Joshua and Nehemiah are once again instructive for leaders.

As mentioned earlier, the Book of Joshua is a story of success and victory. Because of their dependence on God, rarely did the Children of Israel meet defeat. Note the following:

> So the Lord gave Israel all the land he had sworn to give their forefathers, and they took possession of it and settled there. The Lord gave them rest on every side, just as he had sworn to their forefathers. Not one of their enemies withstood them; the Lord handed all their enemies over to them. Not one of all the Lord's good promises to the house of Israel failed; every one was fulfilled (Joshua 21:43-45).

Interestingly, we're also told about how the spoils of victory were allotted to the various tribes. Only after each tribe had received its inheritance did the Israelites turn to the matter of compensating their leader.

> When they had finished dividing the land into its allotted portions, the Israelites gave Joshua son of Nun an inheritance among them, as the Lord had commanded. They gave him the town he asked for—Timnath Serah in the hill country of Ephraim. And he built up the town and settled there (Joshua 19:49-50).

In other words, Joshua did not get his inheritance until after the others, the people he was leading, received theirs. Obviously, current practice is many times just the opposite.

We have previously set forth the story of Nehemiah. He too chose not to receive the "entitlements" as governor.

Moreover, from the twentieth year of King Artaxerxes, when

> I was appointed to be their governor in the land of Judah, until his thirty-second year—twelve years—neither I nor my brothers ate the food allotted to the governor. But the earlier governors—those preceding me—placed a heavy burden on the people and took forty shekels of silver from them in addition to food and wine. Their assistants also lorded it over the people. But out of reverence for God I did not act like that. . . . Instead, I devoted myself to the work on this wall. All my men were assembled there for the work; we did not acquire any land (Nehemiah 5:14-16).

Yes, Nehemiah could have had more, but he chose to have less because he wanted nothing to do with "lording it over the people."

Several other biblical observations might also be of help. The Apostle Peter, for example, reminds us that as leaders we are not to lord our position over those we lead nor are we to be greedy for money:

> Be shepherds of God's flock that is under your care, serving as overseers—not because you must, but because you are willing, as God wants you to be; not greedy for money, but eager to serve; not lording it over those entrusted to you, but being examples to the flock (1 Peter 5:2-3).

Peter also reminds us of leadership's true reward: "And when the Chief Shepherd appears, you will receive the *crown of glory* that will never fade away" (1 Peter 5:4, italics added). Elsewhere, we leaders are told, "Whatever you do, work at it with all your heart, as working for the Lord, not for men" (Colossians 3:23).

The question is legitimately raised: What about the worker? Doesn't he deserve his wages? Good point. After a brief review of the context of Luke 10:7, however, even this interpretation yields to the position stated in 1 Peter and Colossians. Let's look. Jesus, in the process of sending out workers because the "harvest is plentiful but the workers are few" (Luke 10:2), gives these instructions: "Stay in that house, eating and drinking *whatever* they give you, for the worker deserves his wages" (v. 7, italics added). Jesus seems to be saying, "When you go into a house, and they offer you bread and water, accept it with thanks. You deserve it. If you are offered steak and shrimp, accept it with thanks. You deserve it. In other words, whether they offer you something nice or not, enjoy it and accept it with thanks." He's careful not to say, "If they offer you cereal and milk, negotiate for steak and eggs."

This seems to be consistent with Paul's observation in Philippians 4 where, discussing material things, he exhorted his readers to be content in whatever were their circumstances:

> I have learned to be content whatever the circumstances. I know what it is to be in need, and I know what it is to have plenty. I have learned the secret of being content in any and every situation, whether well fed or hungry, whether living in plenty or in want. I can do everything through him who gives me strength (Philippians 4:11-13).

The writer to the Hebrews had a similar thought in mind when he advised, "Keep your lives free from the love of money and be content with what you have, because God has said, 'Never will I leave you; never will I forsake you'" (Hebrews 13:5).

In summary, then, it's difficult to make an argument for the leader negotiating up-front compensation packages. Rather, the model seems to be that, if one feels called by God to a given position, then whatever is offered ought to be accepted; after all, *He has promised* to meet our needs.

TRANSITIONS

Transitions in leadership tend to be awkward at best and divisive at worst—even within Christian organizations. Followers tend to become committed to a given leader and when that person is no longer the leader, for either voluntary or involuntary reasons, a certain amount of organizational tension is inevitable.

Some argue that once a leader retires or is "retired," he should no longer remain in the same geographical area. The reason for this is that if a retired popular leader remains in the same area, people within the organization will not transfer their loyalties to the new leader. The opposing argument, particularly with the case of the retired popular leader, is that since the retired person has built up a residual base of goodwill, his successor proceeds at his own peril if he fails to utilize that expertise for the good of the organization.

As a general operational guideline, transitions in leadership ought not be left to happenstance. Indeed, transitions ought to be well-planned long in advance. In *The Art of Japanese Management*, authors Pascale and Athos list the five key ingredients necessary "to build a great corporation that persists across time, especially after its builders are gone."

It takes first, *a long time.* Second, it takes *constant socialization* of new people and *constant training* of those who keep moving higher. Third, it takes endless articulation and reinforcement of *what the institution honors, values, and believes.* Fourth, it takes *obsessive attention* from the CEO. And fifth, it takes *careful planning* for (leadership) succession long in advance.[1]

Indeed, for transitions to be effective, the goodwill of both the retiring incumbent and the successor leader is essential if the work of the organization is to continue unabated. Some have argued that one of the most important legacies a leader can leave an institution is a smooth transition in leadership, where organizational allegiance can be quickly and readily given to the new leader.

John Gardner argues that a good leader constantly insists that followers will look to their own resources and their own initiatives rather than always look to the leader for direction:

The purposes of the group are best served when the leader helps followers to develop their own initiative, strengthens them in the use of their own judgment, enables them to grow and to become better contributors.[2]

A leader has the option from the beginning of his tenure to decide whether the organization ought to be built around the leader or around the organizational ethos and its people. Gardner convincingly argues for the latter:

To the extent that leaders enable followers to develop their own initiative, they are creating something that can survive their own departure. Some individuals who have dazzling powers of personal leadership not only fail to build institutional strength but create dependency in those below them. However spectacular their personal performance, they leave behind a weakened organization staffed by weakened people. In contrast, leaders who strengthen their people and have a gift for institution-building may create a legacy that will last for a very long time.[3]

Gardner notes that there are leaders "who diminish their followers, rendering them dependent and childlike, exploiting their unconscious need for the god-like magic helper of their infancy."[4] He observes that James Jones of Jonestown worked systematically to obliterate adult judgment and create dependency among his followers.[5] What Gardner is in essence suggesting is that a leader must always be asking the question: what effect will my departure, involuntary or otherwise, have on the continuing stability of the organization? Have I made my constituents or followers so dependent on me that they are unable to support a new leader, whether pastor or president? This consideration, then, leads us back again to the issue of transitions in leadership.

Michael Youssef shares several helpful suggestions on this subject of transitions. First, he notes that "one characteristic of good leaders is that they prepare others to take over. They don't just prepare their followers to 'do well,' but prepare them to do everything they are doing themselves."[6] He further suggests that current leaders help in the process of preparing other leaders by giving others "responsibilities before they're ready for it" and "before they ask for it."[7]

Scripture itself gives us several case studies on leadership transitions. We'll look first at the transition from David to Solomon, then the one from Moses to Joshua, and, finally, the transition from Joshua to literally no one.

DAVID TO SOLOMON. The transition from David to Solomon recorded in 1 Kings was almost a disaster. David had previously told Bathsheba that her son Solomon would be David's successor. Apparently, though, as David got older, he forgot to tell others about his choice! Thus 1 Kings opens with another son of David, Adonijah—a son whom David "had never interfered with by asking, 'Why do you behave as you do?' " (1:6)—declaring himself to be David's successor. Adonijah even gave a party to celebrate his new responsibility. Fortunately, Nathan the prophet shared this news with Bathsheba who subsequently shared it with David, saying: "My lord the king, the eyes of all Israel are on you, to learn from you who will sit on the throne of my lord the king after him" (v. 20). King David responded by clearly announcing to all that Solomon was to be his successor. Civil war was avoided and the transition in leadership then proceeded smoothly.

MOSES TO JOSHUA. In the latter chapters of Deuteronomy, God had made it clear to Moses that he was no longer to be the leader of Israel, and that Joshua was to be his successor. Since we're told that when Moses died, "his eyes were not weak nor his strength gone" (Deuteronomy 34:7), God had other reasons for desiring a new leader. Fortunately, Moses did not fight the changeover but worked hard at making the transition effective. Notice his charge to Joshua:

> Then Moses summoned Joshua and said to him in the presence of all Israel, "Be strong and courageous, for you must go with this people into the land that the Lord swore to their forefathers to give them, and you must divide it among them as their inheritance. The Lord himself goes before you and will be with you; he will never leave you nor forsake you. Do not be afraid; do not be discouraged" (Deuteronomy 31:7-8).

The next step in the transition was that God took Moses out of the picture. After the charge had been given to Joshua, on that same day God spoke to Moses:

> Go up into the Abarim Range to Mount Nebo in Moab, across from Jericho, and view Canaan, the land I am giving the Israelites as their own possession. There on the mountain that you have climbed you will die and be gathered to your people, just as your brother Aaron died on Mount Hor and was gathered to his people. This is because both of you broke faith with me in the presence of the Israelites at the waters of Meribah Kadesh in the Desert of Zin and because you did not uphold my holiness among the Israelites. Therefore, you will see the land only from a distance; you will not enter (Deuteronomy 32:48-52).

In these verses we see not only Moses being taken out of the picture, but we also see the awesome price for failure in leadership.

Finally, we see the positive response of the people to the leadership change:

> Now Joshua son of Nun was filled with the spirit of wisdom because Moses had laid his hands on him. So the Israelites listened to him and did what the Lord had commanded Moses (Deuteronomy 34:9).

> Just as we fully obeyed Moses, so we will obey you. Only may the Lord your God be with you as he was with Moses (Joshua 1:17).

POST-JOSHUA. After the deaths of Joshua and the elders who outlived him, there remained in the succeeding generations no godly men to take the reins of leadership. Chaos resulted:

> After Joshua had dismissed the Israelites, they went to take possession of the land, each to his own inheritance. The people served the Lord throughout the lifetime of Joshua and of the elders who outlived him and who had seen all the great things the Lord had done for Israel. . . . After that whole generation had been gathered to their fathers, another generation grew up, who knew neither the Lord nor what he had done for Israel (Judges 2:6-7, 10).

Joshua had not designated a successor from a younger generation, and the consequences were very tragic for the nation of Israel.

These case studies again reflect the importance of the need for smooth transitions in leadership. The good of the organization depends on it. Leaders must always be aware that the day will eventually arrive when they must step aside from their assigned responsibilities of leadership. When it does, they must be committed to helping the organization move forward despite their departures.

Along with Christ's other disciples, Peter was involved in a multiyear preparation program for a significant transition in leadership, a transition Peter didn't quite fully understand. He failed a significant leadership test during the trial and Crucifixion. Yet

Jesus the leader always believed in Peter and in the rest of His disciples. Not until after the Lord's death and resurrection were they fully aware that He had entrusted His agenda to them. The Book of Acts records their positive response.

Then and now, transitions in leadership continue. The future of the church, and the role that many organizations perform as part of the work of the kingdom, depend on how well these kinds of transitions in leadership are handled.

VULNERABILITY

"Why are leaders so elitist?" It's a question often asked by followers in an organization. Followers want leaders who are reachable, not leaders who are so "high and mighty" that one can't climb the pedestal to reach them. From my perspective, the issue is not so much one of "perceived elitism" as much as it is one of vulnerability. How vulnerable do leaders make themselves to the persons they lead? By *vulnerable*, I don't mean that leaders ought to go around "hanging out" all kinds of soiled laundry. Rather, I mean the ongoing demonstration and expression of basic human qualities, qualities such as anger, disappointment, and pain.

This complex issue has been debated from various perspectives. On the one hand, some argue that it is absolutely essential for leaders to maintain distance between themselves and those they lead. This train of thought is represented by James Fisher and is reflected in the following quote from his book *Power of the Presidency*. Referring to the college and university president, Fisher makes the following observation:

> Distance has characterized effective leaders throughout history. And there need be nothing dishonest or unethical in its practice; it is simply unwise for a college president to establish intimate relationships with members of the faculty he or she must serve.[8]

As the argument is developed, Fisher points out that the people being led refuse to accept the leader as a regular person. Rather, the leader, because he or she holds the power to hire and fire, is someone who is always the president. Accordingly, invitations to social occasions (other than business) are rare. What's more, followers have a tendency to view the leader as "better than I am." In other words, the follower can have a given hang-up or weakness, but the leader had better not have it. Vulnerability, therefore, is to be avoided at all costs for, if the leader is perceived by followers as just a regular person, he may be unfit for leadership. As Fisher observes:

> Leaders are idealized as those whose strength enables them to assume the responsibility for their followers and who can devise better solutions and direction. Indeed, in this idealization, followers deny that leaders experience doubts, insecurities, or weaknesses. Followers react to their leaders' human foibles with astonishment, dismay, and even anger to an exaggerated degree, as if to say, "If you are not totally dependable, then you may not be dependable at all."[9]

The leader, in this view, is in a Catch-22. According to Pascale and Athos, Japanese managers are more apt to exhibit vulnerability than are their Western counterparts:

> He is more likely to reveal his weaknesses and idiosyncrasies to his subordinates. In fact, many Japanese managers feel that by revealing their vulnerabilities they are better able to enlist assistance. Contrast this to subordinates in the West, who often have to discern a superior's weakness through a veneer of pseudocompetence. We are often inhibited from directly offering to help a boss because we are supposed to accept the "superior" image he is trying so hard to portray.[10]

If distance is maintained, the leader may be perceived as aloof and arrogant. If the leader becomes vulnerable, and shares weaknesses and other human tendencies, he's not worth following. Every leader has experienced this tension and seeming paradox.

On the other end of the spectrum is the position that it's OK for a leader to be vulnerable. Psychologist James Carr represents this viewpoint:

> As a premise of leadership, "familiarity breeds contempt" is a cop-out. It may serve a purpose, but does it serve the cause of leadership? By waving your degrees, your rank, your

authority in the face of your subordinates and keeping them at arm's length, you can avoid the bother of knowing them . . . or caring about them. You can prevent their knowledge or caring about you as well and thus evade the responsibility that involvement implies. But what is teamwork without involvement?[11]

There seems to be little question that Scripture gives us a picture of Christians working together to reflect the bodily qualities of unity or teamwork. Certainly this concept of working together in unity is conducive to encouraging vulnerability in leadership. Note, for example, the following New Testament references:

> If you have any encouragement from being united with Christ, if any comfort from his love, if any fellowship with the Spirit, if any tenderness and compassion, then make my joy complete by being like-minded, having the same love, being one in spirit and purpose. Do nothing out of selfish ambition or vain conceit, but in humility consider others better than yourselves (Philippians 2:1-3).

> Finally, all of you, live in harmony with one another; be sympathetic, love as brothers, be compassionate and humble (1 Peter 3:8).

> May the God who gives endurance and encouragement give you a spirit of unity among yourselves as you follow Christ Jesus (Romans 15:5).

> Be devoted to one another in brotherly love. Honor one another above yourselves (Romans 12:10).

As a leader reviewing these verses, I ask myself this question: do these passages and scores of others like them suggest vulnerability or distance? The answer, to me at least, seems rather clear— when Christians are working together, as is the case in the Christian organization, vulnerability, not distance, ought to be the operative expectation. Indeed, in Paul's letter to the Galatians, he instructed them as follows: "Carry each other's burdens, and in this way you will fulfill the law of Christ" (Galatians 6:2).
Bearing someone else's burdens in a corporate context pre-

supposes each party has knowledge of those burdens. And if I'm not practicing vulnerability, then both I and the people I lead will not be able to practice what Scripture asks me to do.

But wait. We are not yet done with this matter because, however much desired, simplification of issues doesn't always carry the day. I have seen Christian organizations immobilized because leaders have made themselves vulnerable to followers. The followers then proceeded to discharge the leader. As Jerry White has observed, "People in ministry become closed because they have had friendships betrayed. They share their heart with somebody and say, 'We are really struggling in our marriage or with this or that' and before they know it, the board starts inquiring."[12] Further, would many people in the typical church respond positively if the pastor, on a given Sunday morning, announced that he's been struggling with the issue of lust and desires prayer support? Many in the congregation would be shocked that the pastor is as human as they are. Thus the necessity for guidelines that govern when and how the leader makes himself vulnerable. Several suggestions follow.

For starters, and as previously noted, leaders ought to reflect characteristics of humanness in how they relate to those they lead. They ought to feel their people's hurt, their pain, and their sorrow. Conversely, followers ought to sense the same from their leaders. In the account of Jesus raising Lazarus from the dead, Jesus was touched with the sorrow experienced by the grieving family and "he wept" (John 11:35).

Second, being vulnerable with the more personal struggles of life doesn't mean that "everybody" need know of them. Just as most other people don't share "everything with everybody," leaders nevertheless ought to be regularly in touch with a small group of friends who can both share burdens and insist on accountability. It may not be necessary that this accountability group come from within the organization. It could, in fact, consist of people from different locations. It is vital, however, for the leader to have such people in his life to help share burdens. The leader in isolation is a leader in trouble. The leader's spouse can also be a tremendous advantage in this area—as long as the marriage relationship is solid and as long as one spouse feels that the other values and can handle honest opinions and reactions.

Finally, and again as previously noted, it doesn't follow that vulnerability means "explicit garbage dumping." Leaders need to exercise discretion in sharing details. Asking for prayer regarding the "fight he and his spouse had" might reflect the actual experience, but it might be just as effective to request prayer for "learning to love my wife better." After all, God knows *all* the details and some are better left to Him.

CHAPTER FOURTEEN

LONELINESS AND LEADERSHIP— THE SPOUSE'S VIEW

•

This chapter represents yet another side of leadership—the view of the leader's spouse. It focuses on the issue of spousal loneliness and how to deal with it. What follows is an article reprinted in its entirety from the *United Brethren* magazine.[1]

Excitement filled the air as people gathered for the festivities. The occasion? The inauguration of the 11th president of Huntington College.

The inaugural address was powerfully delivered—"For Such a Time as This," from Esther. Then came applause, congratulations, handshakes, supportive words. That day, Gene and I were flooded with joy as we began this new adventure, this next step in God's plan for our family.

I eagerly accepted my new role as president's wife, confident that I would make the transition smoothly. How naive I was. A few months later, reality struck.

JOY AND DISAPPOINTMENT

After running errands one beautiful spring day, I returned to find the florist's truck parked in our driveway. The delivery man gave me a colorful array of helium balloons.

I opened the note. It said, "Just to let you know you and your family are greatly appreciated." It was from a woman who knew we were undergoing tremendous pressure related to The Job.

I immediately called and thanked her. Then I asked, "Would you be interested in coming for lunch today?"

She hesitated a moment before saying, "OK."

I scurried around preparing a simple lunch to serve on the deck overlooking Lake Sno-Tip. I got out my best china and silver. Everything looked perfect.

The time passed. 1:00 . . . 1:30 . . . 2:00 . . . 2:15. The doorbell never chimed.

Finally, realizing she was not coming, I called.

"I'm sorry, I couldn't get away," she began quietly. Then she admitted, "I must be honest. I can't let people see my car in your driveway because. . . ."

On she went, but I heard little else. "Yes, I understand," I responded politely. But inside, I screamed, *I don't care what other people think!*

I was crushed. I slowly covered the salads, brought in the flowers, folded the cloth napkins, and gathered the dinnerware. Then, sitting down with a cup of coffee, I cried and cried.

FALLOUT FROM THE JOB

It wasn't the first time people had distanced themselves from me. Soon after we came to Huntington, a woman approached me and matter-of-factly said, "We appreciate you and your family and will be friends. But we will never come to your home. People might think we are becoming too close, and it could interfere with the working relationship."

People stopped just "popping in" for a visit, especially after Gene assumed the presidency and we moved into the new president's home. And I realized that my own "popping in" on people made many feel uncomfortable.

Personnel changes at the college sometimes dramatically affected relationships. I had been ignored, glared at. One time, when I met someone head-on in the grocery store, the person made a 180-degree turn and walked the other way.

I couldn't blame any of these people—not really. I knew it wasn't their fault. It was The Job. Being the college president's wife, I had to endure a certain amount of isolation. And that, in turn, produced some loneliness. I felt like I was losing my ability to be a friend.

As I sipped my coffee, I picked up a spoon and stared at it.

From a distance, the spoon glistened in the sunlight. But up close, I could clearly see a tarnish spot I had missed.

How like people in leadership positions, I thought.

Business executives, politicians, pastors, parachurch heads, denominational officials—I knew that these people and their spouses shared some of the feelings I experienced as a college president's wife. *My, what a special person*, we think upon seeing someone shining in the limelight. But stop, look closer, peer more intently—there's a dark spot, and another. Tarnish stains the gleaming silver.

For me, loneliness was one of those spots. I needed to find a special kind of polish and some soft cloths so I could gently rub away the stain. Then I could shine on and do the work God had called me to do.

UNDERSTANDING LONELINESS

The best way to begin dealing with the problem is to examine its causes. So, I began studying loneliness.

I talked to people in similar leadership positions. I spoke with counselors. And I read as much as I could on the subject. I began learning a great deal about loneliness.

ROLE EXPECTATIONS. Loneliness is an emotion which is difficult to describe. It hurts. It is a gnawing feeling, like a dull ache before the flu strikes. Someone described it as a cold gray mist that filters around your heart and soul. I could identify with that mist; after living four years in Portland, Oregon, I knew all about cold gray mist.

The Bible told me that God anticipated the pain of loneliness. "It is not good for the man to be alone," He said in Genesis 2:18. He created us with a desire for fellowship.

Continuing in my search, I learned that all people experience loneliness. However, some causes are peculiar to those in leadership positions.

Craig Ellison, in his book *Saying Good-Bye to Loneliness*, discusses the "role isolation" of leaders. Because of your title or position, people relate to you differently. They may hold certain expectations, or view you as an invulnerable hero or spiritual giant.

One time, after addressing a women's group, I went to the back of the room to greet people. One woman took my hand and, staring at me intently, said, "Well, you don't look like a president's wife."

Do you know how uncomfortable that made me feel? I ran through a mental checklist of my appearance. Was my hair too short or too long? Should I have worn my black suit? I was a victim of role expectations, boxes.

Ellison says the isolation comes from the *role*, not the *person* in the role. For instance, the balloons were sent to the *person*, but the lunch was canceled because of the *role*.

I discovered several other sources of loneliness.

JOB FUNCTION. The function of the job can cause isolation. The higher your position, the more privileged information flows across your desk. You must remain silent on certain subjects to maintain confidentiality, avoid leaks, or prevent distortions. Other people, misinterpreting your silence, may conclude, "He thinks he's too good for us," or, "She doesn't have any problems."

LACK OF TIME. People in leadership have great demands on their time. Although you try to juggle your schedule to maintain intimate friendships, they may not understand why you can't spend much time with them anymore.

"She's too busy for me, so I won't be a part of her life."

Or, "I'm not a *person* in her life. I'm just another item on her agenda."

You cry out, "Please, I need you. Try to understand." Some do, but some don't.

MOBILITY. We moved nine times in the first thirteen years of our marriage. It hurts to pull up roots, sever friendships, leave family. After many moves, you begin wondering, "Should I even bother putting down roots and making new friends?"

The better choice is to take the risk of being yanked out again, and enjoy the persons God places in your life for that place and time.

LOOKING INWARD

In my search, I realized that all of these things were *job*-related. The next step was more painful: looking at sources that were self-related.

I asked myself some tough questions. Do I like myself? Do I have good self-esteem? Do I know how I fit into the overall team ministry?

Although I had earned a Masters degree, I chose to set aside a career to be the support system for a very busy husband. Sometimes, I felt like just an ornament on his lapel. But in reality, I was a valuable asset.

"Are you teaching this year?" someone asked me.

"No," I answered.

"Well, are you substituting?"

"No."

The next question was a killer. "Then what do you do all day?"

That question bugged me. What *do* I do all day? I decided to keep a log for two weeks, writing down everything I did. I found I did *lots* of things—shopping, car-pooling, attending board meetings, ministering to others, cleaning out the fireplace soot one hour to prepare for an elegant banquet the next, hosting surprise guests, serving lunch to 150 people on our lawn, giving a child's pet rabbit eyedrops . . .

I was fulfilled. This was my job, my place of contentment—my source of identity and self-worth apart from my husband.

THE ETERNAL FRIEND

How is my relationship with God? I asked myself. I didn't want to consider this as a possible cause of loneliness, but I had to. A weakened relationship with the Father can allow loneliness to flood in.

A few years before, when I was feeling the blues, I had called a friend in Maryland and shared my discontent. She listened for a while, and then asked, "How's your relationship with God right now?"

My first reaction was, *It's none of your business.* But after a few seconds, I gave her an honest answer: "It's not very good."

Now, I considered her question again. I realized I was busy spending time *for* the Lord, but not spending enough time *with* the Lord. That had to change.

TENDING THE TEMPLE

I identified one more area: physical fitness. If I wasn't eating properly or getting enough exercise, I would suffer mentally and emotionally—and that can start the cycle of depression and loneliness. I decided to get a physical and look at my diet.

TAKING ACTION

Throughout my investigation, I wrote down my innermost feelings. As I learned about loneliness and why it occurs, I noticed a healing taking place.

But much work remained.

When I notice a tarnish spot on a piece of my good silver, I have two choices. *One,* I can pretend it's not there, avoid looking at it, or hide it in a cupboard. Or *two,* I can choose the right cleaner and, step by step, gently rub the spot away and see the beautiful shine return.

So it is with loneliness. We can pretend it's not there—and allow it to get worse. Or we can deal with it. The Lord will help us, but there are things we can do too. Three areas especially need our attention. They regard God, self, and others.

COMMUNION WITH GOD. A close relationship with the Lord is the most important cure for loneliness.

Lloyd Ogilvie, in his book *The Bush Is Still Burning,* describes loneliness as "homesickness for God." The world's antidote for loneliness, he says, is to join more groups, travel, shop, eat, change spouses. But when the activity stops and the people leave, the hurt remains. God created us with a longing for Him that no person or thing can satisfy.

"Be still and know that I am God," wrote the psalmist. "In quietness and confidence is your strength," added Isaiah.

In *The Celebration of Discipline,* Richard Foster distinguishes between loneliness and aloneness. He describes loneliness as inner emptiness, a preoccupation with "poor me—I am all alone and so blue." Aloneness, on the other hand, is inner fulfillment—"Now that I am alone with Jesus, I can recover, repair, and regroup."

SELF-IMAGE. We must dare to stretch and grow, to escape from our ruts. It's scary to reach out in a new area. But the joy of accomplishing something makes it all worthwhile.

A related area is goal-setting. We desperately need short-term and long-term goals to give us direction, something to get up for each day.

My husband has helped me with this. He is very goal-oriented and task-driven; I, by nature, am neither. He knows what he will do for the next ten years; I know what I will have for dinner tonight. Really, I am getting much better, but this area still needs much work.

Another way to enhance your self-image is to join an image-improvement class. If the outer self needs some work, maybe you should get serious about shedding those few pounds. Working on the outer image helps build the inner image.

In any case, always remember that you are very valuable to God and uniquely made. Don't try to fit other people's expectations. Be yourself—that is the way God intended you to function in the world—and live according to the beat of His drum, not of others'.

REACHING OUT. When I asked people in leadership how they deal with loneliness, the same answer kept surfacing: "Do something for someone else."

Many times, when I have felt the cold gray chill of loneliness approaching, I have bought one solitary rose and taken it to someone God laid on my heart—someone else who needed cheering up that day. It's a wonderful healing balm.

Do you desire close friends? Then you must take the initiative. Friendships don't develop by sitting back and waiting for people to come to you.

A president's wife from a nearby college told me she used to wait for the phone to ring, hoping someone would invite her to lunch. It rarely happened. But when she began taking the initiative, some special relationships bloomed. It takes time; it involves risk; it means being vulnerable. But it works.

A woman once expressed her loneliness and lack of friends to Henrietta Mears, the great Christian educator.

"What qualities do you want in a friend?" Mears asked her.

She responded, "Someone who would accept me, not misuse me. Someone I could count on in spite of everything, and who would share my hopes and dreams."

Mears said, "Go, be that friend to other people. You will find that that is what they will be to you." Good advice.

We all need people with whom we can talk on a deep level, beyond surface concerns. Some people need several such friendships, others maybe just one (in which case it should be your spouse). But everyone needs someone. If you don't have an intimate friend, ask God to send someone into your life.

And what about the people who won't let you close to them, perhaps because of your role?

This is difficult for me. I'm such a lover of people. I've always wanted to please people, to make hurts "all better," to never have anyone angry with me.

But sometimes, this isn't possible. Regardless of how people respond to me, my responsibility is to *love* them and speak with them and *love* them and pray for them and *love* them—with the love of Jesus.

A FORMULA FOR PEACE

Now let's take some soft cloths and begin rubbing in the polish. For me, the cloths represent praise. Praise to the Heavenly Father inoculates us against Satan, who doesn't want us to shine, succeed, or be faithful in using God's gifts. He gains the upper hand by making us discouraged and downcast, because we can't praise and complain at the same time.

Last summer my 10-year-old daughter, Marybeth, went to camp—her first time away from home. Before leaving, she cried every night, knowing she would miss us terribly. We tried to dispel her fears, but to no avail.

Then we called Grandma. As Marybeth heard Grandma's voice, her eyes grew large like saucers and a smile crossed her face. Tightening her eyes, she prayed with Grandma and then hung up the phone.

"I've got it!" she squealed with delight. "I know why I've been feeling so bad! Grandma said Satan doesn't want me to go to camp because I'll learn about Jesus all week! I just need to tell him to get lost!"

That is exactly what she did. There wasn't another tear.

Satan doesn't want us to succeed, to grow, to be close to the Lord. He will use our weak spots to tear us down. We need to use praise and thanks even when we don't even feel like it, because they break the stronghold of Satan in our lives.

Is there tarnish on your silver which needs to be removed? Begin by going to Jesus. Then pour effort into doing things that will pull you up. The tarnish in our lives can be rubbed away so that we shine for Him.

CONCLUSION

Leading and following, as we used the terms, are incredibly important to the future prospects of any organization. As this book has attempted to show, however, leading and following, required of all who participate in an organization, are functions not easily carried out.

We began this book by reviewing and discussing the idea of leadership and its related concepts, including those of power and authority. As we noted, leaders can't lead without having authority and leaders can't possess authority without having power. As Stott has noted:

> A certain authority attaches to all leaders, and leadership would be impossible without it. . . . Leaders have power, but power is safe only in the hands of those who humble themselves to serve.[1]

The issue, then, in leading, is not "power versus authority" but rather how power and authority have been acquired, how they are being handled within the organization, and, further, the ends to which they are applied.

For the Christian leader who leads and follows—and one must be both to be effective—both the process of leading and the "ends" of leading are extremely important. Leaders must be neither masters nor bosses. Stott has observed:

Among the followers of Jesus, therefore, leadership is not a synonym for lordship. Our calling is to be servants not bosses, slaves not masters. . . . The emphasis of Jesus was not on the authority of the ruler-leader but on the humility of a servant-leader.[2]

And as John White has noted:

The true leader serves. Serves people. Serves their best interests, and in so doing will not always be popular, may not always impress. But because true leaders are motivated by loving concern rather than a desire for personal glory, they are willing to pay the price.[3]

Many times, and in some organizations, an emphasis on servant leadership produces no action, or stagnation, in the leader-follower (or constituent) relationship. As a result, the organization ceases to exist—or if it continues to exist, serves no useful purpose. Alternatively, what we have tried to say in this book is that an effective leader, even though a servant of the people, nevertheless helps keep the people moving on a given course or direction. The shepherd, for example, doesn't serve the sheep well if the flock is permitted to move randomly in all directions at will. Gardner comments:

The leader-constituent relationship is at best mutually nourishing, mutually strengthening. It is not a bland relationship. It is not without tension and conflict. . . . The ideal is leadership strong enough to propose clear directions and followers strong enough to criticize and amend—and finally, enough continuity of purpose to resolve disputes and move on.[4]

Further, we have tried to emphasize that effective organizational leadership, within the context of an organization's purpose or mission, must have a healthy preoccupation with the people of the organization. As Gardner has noted, "We believe, with Immanuel Kant, that individuals should be treated as ends in themselves, not as means to the leader's ends."[5] Indeed, people in the organization are critically important to the organization's goals.

Whether one deals with the burdens of leadership, the priorities of perspective and excellence, the matters of confrontation and forgiveness, or other organizational issues, the leader must retain a primary concern and focus for the people being led. As I have attempted to show, this goal is best carried out when centered on biblical principles.

In Rosabeth Moss Kanter's book, *The Change Masters*, she provides yet another reason for a leadership focus on the people within an organization. Organizations need new ideas to survive, and "the source of new ideas is people."[6] As she notes, there are too many organization problems and too few ideas resident within the organization to address them—unless leadership "frees up" human potential toward that end:

> There are not enough creative geniuses to go around and there are too many problems in most American companies in this era for them to be able to afford to have only a handful of people thinking about solutions.[7]

She then provides this startling reminder:

> The true "tragedy" for most declining American companies struggling to keep afloat . . . is not how far they are from the potential for transformation but how close they might come and not know it.[8]

Thus, we have come full circle. Christian leaders have long known of their biblical responsibility to be committed to the people they lead. What we need to continually remind ourselves is that failure to adhere to these biblical priorities also deprives the organization of its opportunity to achieve its potential.

In conclusion, organizations need leaders—a certain kind of leader—after all. We don't need the kind of leaders John White describes: "petrified little people who dream of power."[9] Rather, we need godly men and women who are wholeheartedly committed to serving both God and the people within the organizations they lead. These leaders may not be in great abundance, but they have always been there and are appearing in a growing number of organizations.

These kinds of leaders "are meant to be facilitators not

despots . . . [and] they must use their authority in the way Jesus did."[10]

As White has noted:

There has always been a true elite of God's leaders. They are the meek who inherit the earth (Matthew 5:5). They weep and pray in secret, and defy earth and hell in public. They tremble when faced with danger, but die in their tracks sooner than turn back. They are like a shepherd defending his sheep or a mother protecting her young. They sacrifice without grumbling, give without calculating, suffer without groaning. To those in their charge they say, "We live well if you do well." Their price is above riches. They are the salt of the earth.[11]

For the cause of the kingdom, we need more of them.

NOTES

Introduction
1. Robert Lindsey, "Religious Sects, Powerful Leaders Gain in Popularity," *The Fort Wayne Journal-Gazette*, Sunday, June 29, 1986, p. 7A.
2. *The Chronicle of Higher Education*, May 28, 1986, p. 20.
3. See Cheryl Forbes, *The Religion of Power* (Grand Rapids, Mich.: Zondervan Publishing House, 1983), p. 66 and Michael Maccoby, *The Leader* (New York: Simon & Schuster, 1981), p. 219.
4. Michael Maccoby, *The Leader* (New York: Simon & Schuster, 1981), pp. 17, 13.
5. Frank Goble, *Excellence in Leadership* (Caroline House Publishers, 1972), p. 34.
6. John H. Yoder, *He Came Preaching Peace* (Scottsdale, Pa.: Herald Press, 1985), p. 104.

Chapter 1—Preliminary Considerations of Leadership
1. *The Chronicle of Higher Education*, May 28, 1986, p. 20.
2. *Ibid.*
3. See Frank Goble, *Excellence in Leadership* (Caroline House Publishers, 1972), p. 6 and Stanley O. Ikenberry, "1990: A President's Perspective," *Planning*, vol. 14, no. 3 (1986), p. 2.
4. Donald E. Walker, "Administrators v. Faculty," *Change*, March/April, 1986, p. 9.
5. Robert K. Mossie, Jr., "Prophets to Profits," *Best of Business Quarterly*, vol. 8, no. 1, Spring, 1986, p. 15.
6. John W. Gardner, *The Nature of Leadership* (Washington, D.C.: Independent Sector, 1986), pp. 25-26.
7. *Ibid.*, pp. 9, 12.

8. Ikenberry, *op. cit.*, p. 3.
9. Gardner, *op. cit.*, p. 6.
10. *Ibid.*, p. 6.
11. *Ibid.*
12. "Followership," *Christian Leadership Letter*, September, 1986.
13. Gardner, *op.cit.*, p. 6.
14. *Ibid.*, p. 7.
15. *Ibid.*, p. 8.
16. John W. Gardner, *The Tasks of Leadership* (Washington, D.C.: Independent Sector, 1986), p. 5.
17. *Ibid.*, p. 7.
18. *Ibid.*
19. *Ibid.*, p. 9.
20. *Ibid.*
21. *Ibid.*, p. 10.
22. *Ibid.*, p. 13.
23. *Ibid.*
24. *Ibid.*, p. 15.
25. *Ibid.*, p. 18.
26. *Ibid.*, p. 19.
27. *Ibid.*
28. *Ibid.*
29. *Ibid.*, p. 20.
30. *Ibid.*, p. 22.
31. John W. Gardner, *Self-Renewal* (New York: Harper & Row, 1963, 1964), p. 58.
32. John W. Gardner, *The Nature of Leadership* (Washington, D.C.: Independent Sector, 1986), p. 15.
33. *Ibid.*, p. 16.
34. Daniel Katz and Robert L. Kahn, *The Social Psychology of Organizations, 2nd ed.* (New York: John Wiley & Sons, 1978), p. 527.
35. *Ibid.*
36. *Ibid.*, p. 528.
37. *Ibid.*, p. 532.
38. *Ibid.*, p. 533.
39. *Ibid.*
40. *Ibid.*, p. 536.
41. *Ibid.*, pp. 540-547.
42. *Ibid.*, p. 545.
43. *Ibid.*, p. 546.
44. David Whetten, "Effective Administrators," *Change*, November/December, 1984, p. 40.
45. Katz and Kahn, *op. cit.*, p. 546.
46. *Ibid.*, p. 534.
47. *Ibid.*
48. *Ibid.*, p. 535.
49. *Ibid.*
50. *Ibid.*, p. 569.

51. *Ibid.*
52. *Ibid.*, p. 571.
53. *Ibid.*

Chapter 2—Power, Authority, and Trust
1. Fremont E. Kast and James E. Rosenzweig, *Organization and Management* (New York: McGraw-Hill, 1974), p. 333.
2. *Ibid.*
3. *Ibid.*
4. *Ibid.*, p. 334.
5. John W. Gardner, *Leadership and Power* (Washington, D.C.: Independent Sector, 1986), p. 3.
6. *Ibid.*, p. 4.
7. *Ibid.*, p. 3.
8. *Ibid.*, p. 5.
9. *Ibid.*, p. 19.
10. *Ibid.*, p. 21.
11. *Ibid.*, p. 19.
12. Richard Foster, *Money, Sex, and Power* (San Francisco: Harper & Row, 1985), pp. 178-179.
13. *Ibid.*, p. 179.
14. Cheryl Forbes, *The Religion of Power* (Grand Rapids, Mich.: Zondervan Publishing House, 1983), p. 87.
15. Richard T. Pascale and Anthony G. Athos, *The Art of Japanese Management* (New York: Warner Books, 1981), p. 243.
16. Forbes, *op. cit.*, p. 151.
17. *Ibid.*, p. 87.
18. Steve Dennie, "The Perils of Power," *The United Brethren*, November, 1983, p. 16.
19. Forbes, *op. cit.*, p. 87.
20. Charles Colson, *Who Speaks for God?* (Westchester, Ill.: Crossway Books, 1985), p. 40.
21. *Ibid.*, p. 41.
22. Kast and Rosenzweig, *op. cit.*, p. 331.
23. *Ibid.*, p. 338.
24. *Ibid.*
25. *Ibid.*
26. *Ibid.*, p. 339.
27. John W. Gardner, *The Nature of Leadership* (Washington, D.C.: Independent Sector, 1986), p. 7.
28. John White and Ken Blue, *Healing the Wounded* (Downers Grove, Ill.: InterVarsity Press, 1985), p. 36.
29. Pascale and Athos, *op. cit.*, p. 246.
30. *Webster's Seventh New Collegiate Dictionary* (Springfield, Mass.: G. & C. Merriam Co., 1970), pp. 952-953.
31. John W. Gardner, *The Heart of the Matter* (Washington, D.C.: Independent Sector, 1986), p. 11.

32. *Ibid.*, p. 18.
33. Louis B. Barnes, "Managing the Paradox of Organizational Trust," *Harvard Business Review* (March-April, 1981), p. 108.
34. *Ibid.*
35. Pascale and Athos, *op. cit.*, p. 126.
36. *Ibid.*, p. 129.
37. Barnes, *op. cit.*, p. 110.
38. *Ibid.*, p. 112.
39. *Ibid.*, p. 114.
40. Gardner, *op. cit.*, p. 19.
41. *Ibid.*

Chapter 3—Chosen by God
1. J. Oswald Sanders, *Spiritual Leadership* (Chicago: Moody Press, 1980), p. 15.

Chapter 4—The Burden of Leadership
1. Lawrence M. Miller, *American Spirit: Visions of a New Corporate Culture* (New York: William Morrow and Company, Inc., 1984), p. 15.
2. John Stott, *Involvement: Social and Sexual Relationships in the Modern World, Vol. II* (Old Tappan, N.J.: Fleming H. Revell Company, 1984, 1985), p. 249.
3. Charles Colson, *Who Speaks for God?* (Westchester, Ill.: Crossway Books, 1985), p. 20.

Chapter 5—Followership
1. John W. Gardner, *The Moral Aspect of Leadership* (Washington, D.C.: Independent Sector, 1987), p. 9.
2. "Followership," *Christian Leadership Letter*, September, 1986, p. 1.
3. Elihu Katz and Paul Lazarsfeld, *Personal Influence* (Glencoe, Ill.: The Free Press, 1955).
4. *Ibid.*, p. 137.
5. John W. Gardner, *The Heart of the Matter* (Washington, D.C.: Independent Sector, 1986), p. 5.
6. *Ibid.*, p. 6.
7. *Ibid.*
8. *Ibid.*
9. *Ibid.*, pp. 8-9.
10. *Ibid.*, p. 10.
11. *Ibid.*, p. 12.
12. Gardner, *The Moral Aspect of Leadership*, *op. cit.*, p. 11.
13. Richard T. Pascale and Anthony G. Athos, *The Art of Japanese Management* (New York: Warner Books, 1981).
14. *Ibid.*, p. 199.

15. *Ibid.*, p. 246.
16. John H. Yoder, *He Came Preaching Peace* (Scottsdale, Pa.: Herald Press, 1985), pp. 20, 46, 91, 130.
17. "Followership," *op. cit.*, p. 1.
18. *Ibid.*, p. 2.
19. *Ibid.*
20. *Ibid.*
21. *Ibid.*
22. *Ibid.*, p. 3.
23. *Ibid.*
24. *Ibid.*
25. Gardner, *The Heart of the Matter, op. cit.*, p. 15.
26. *Ibid.*
27. *Ibid.*
28. *Ibid.*
29. "Academic Culture Said to Discourage Strong Presidency," *The Chronicle of Higher Education*, March 12, 1986, p. 30.
30. "Christian Catchers," *Christian Leadership Letter*, November, 1986, p. 3.
31. "Followership," *op. cit.*, p. 3.

Chapter 6—Confrontation

1. Fred Smith, *Learning to Lead* (Waco, Texas: Word Books, 1986), p. 104.
2. David Augsburger, *Caring Enough to Confront* (Ventura, Calif.: Regal Books, 1973).
3. Daniel Katz and Robert L. Kahn, *The Social Psychology of Organizations, 2nd ed.* (New York: John Wiley & Sons, 1978), p. 571.

Chapter 7—Forgiveness

1. Charles Colson, *Who Speaks for God?* (Westchester, Ill.: Crossway Books, 1985), pp. 136-137.
2. *Ibid.*, p. 137.
3. *Ibid.*, p. 139.

Chapter 8—Planning, Perspective, and Leadership

1. Special mention is made of Dr. Paul Michelson, professor of history and assistant to the president for special projects at Huntington College, who helped develop the ideas and concepts presented in this chapter.
2. John White, *Excellence in Leadership* (Downers Grove, Ill.: Inter-Varsity Press, 1986), pp. 47-48.

Chapter 9—Excellence and Leadership

1. Gary Inrig, *A Call to Excellence* (Wheaton, Ill.: Victor Books, 1985), p. 11.
2. Thomas J. Peters and Robert H. Waterman, Jr., *In Search of Excellence* (New York, Warner Books, 1982).
3. *Ibid.*, p. 26.
4. John W. Gardner, *Excellence* (New York: Harper & Brothers, 1961).
5. John W. Gardner, *Self-Renewal* (New York: Harper & Row, 1963, 1964).
6. *Excellence, op. cit.*, pp. 127-128.
7. *Ibid.*, p. 86.
8. *Ibid.*, pp. 131, 133.
9. Inrig, *op. cit.*, p. 36.
10. *Self-Renewal, op. cit.*, p. 101.
11. *Ibid.*, pp. 54-55.
12. Anthony Campolo, *The Success Fantasy* (Wheaton, Ill.: Victor Books, 1980).
13. Robert T. Sandin, *The Search for Excellence* (Macon, Ga.: Mercer University Press, 1982).
14. *Ibid.*, p. 4.
15. Inrig, *op. cit.*
16. Jon Johnston, *Christian Excellence* (Grand Rapids, Mich.: Baker Book House, 1985).
17. Inrig, *op. cit.*, p. 25.
18. *Ibid.*, p. 27.
19. *Ibid.*, p. 28.
20. *Ibid.*, p. 31.
21. *Ibid.*, p. 32.
22. Johnston, *op. cit.*, p. 30.
23. *Ibid.*, p. 33.
24. *Self-Renewal, op. cit.*, p. 58.
25. Edith Schaeffer, *What Is a Family?* (Old Tappan, N.J.: Fleming H. Revell Company, 1975), p. 32.

Chapter 10—The Leader as Fund-Raiser

1. See Murray L. Bob, "The Bureaucratization of Begging," *The Grantsmanship Center News*, November/December, 1983, p. 49.
2. John White, *The Golden Cow* (Downers Grove, Ill.: InterVarsity Press, 1979), pp. 113-114.
3. Patti Roberts, *Ashes to Gold* (Waco, Texas: Word Books, 1983), p. 107.
4. Edward J. Hales and J. Alan Youngren, *Your Money/Their Ministry* (Grand Rapids, Mich: William B. Eerdmans Co., 1981), pp. 36-50. See also, Bruce K. Waltke, "Why Pray?" *Regent College Quarterly Bulletin*, vol. 13, no. 4, Winter, 1983, and George Barna, "Profile Attitudes of Christian Parachurch Group Donors," *Fund Raising Management*, February, 1985, p. 52: "Among the dominant evangelical radio

programs is James Dobson's 'Focus on the Family' [which] ...brought in $6.8 million in 1983. Direct mail is the primary income source of other organizations—such as American Bible Society or The Navigators—with revenues climbing as high as $40 million annually."

5. Hales and Youngren, *op. cit.*, p. 22: "Unlike foreign missionaries and any other Christian workers ... the Christian broadcaster develops an 'exchange' relationship with those to whom he appeals for funds."
6. White, *op. cit.*, pp. 114-115.
7. Quoted in Steve Dennie, "Tricks of the Fund-Raising Trade" *United Brethren*, 98 (November, 1983), p. 17. The entire issue of the November, 1983, issue of the *United Brethren* (subtitled "They Want Your Money") is recommended reading.
8. White, *op. cit.*, p. 94.
9. See, for example, Luke 14:12-14.
10. Roberts, *op. cit.*, p. 108.
11. *Ibid.*, p. 111.
12. Hales and Youngren, *op. cit.*, p. 7.
13. White, *op. cit.*, pp. 100-101.
14. Catherine Marshall, *Beyond Our Selves* (New York: McGraw-Hill, 1961), pp. 74-81.

Chapter 11—How Much Is Enough?
1. Jeremy Rifkin, *Algeny* (New York: The Viking Press, 1983), pp. 72-73.
2. *Ibid.*, p. 74.
3. *Ibid.*, p. 79.
4. John White, *The Golden Cow* (Downers Grove, Ill.: InterVarsity Press, 1979), pp. 112-113.
5. Rifkin, *op. cit.*, p. 83.
6. *Ibid.*, p. 82.
7. *Ibid.*
8. *Ibid.*, p. 91.
9. John H. Yoder, *He Came Preaching Peace* (Scottsdale, Pa.: Herald Press, 1985), p. 52.
10. Cheryl Forbes, *The Religion of Power* (Grand Rapids, Mich.: Zondervan Publishing House, 1983), p. 29.
11. Rifkin, *op. cit.*, p. 103.
12. Yoder, *op. cit.*, p. 126.
13. Charles Colson, *Who Speaks for God?* (Westchester, Ill.: Crossway Books, 1985), pp. 27, 29.
14. E.M. Bounds, *Power Through Prayer* (Grand Rapids, Mich.: Baker Book House, 1972), p. 60.
15. *Ibid.*, p. 125.
16. *Ibid.*
17. Rifkin, *op. cit.*, p. 254.

18. Bounds, *op. cit.*, p. 114.

Chapter 12—Leadership—The Personal Dimension
1. Larry Richards, *The Screw-Loose Letters* (Waco, Texas: Word Books, 1980).
2. J. Oswald Sanders, "Lessons I've Learned," *Discipleship Journal*, Issue Fifteen, p. 14.
3. John Stott, *Involvement: Social and Sexual Relationships in the Modern World, Vol. II* (Old Tappan, N.J.: Fleming H. Revell Company, 1984, 1985), p. 216.
4. Name Withheld, "The War Within: An Anatomy of Lust," *Leadership*, Fall, 1982, vol. III, no. 4, pp. 30-48.
5. Cheryl Forbes, *The Religion of Power* (Grand Rapids, Mich.: Zondervan Publishing House, 1983), p. 73.
6. Stott, *op. cit.*, p. 215.
7. Forbes, *op. cit.*, p. 79.
8. Richard T. Pascale and Anthony G. Athos, *The Art of Japanese Management* (New York: Warner Books, 1981), p. 218.
9. Forbes, *op. cit.*, p. 75.
10. *Ibid.*
11. Richard J. Foster, *Money, Sex and Power* (San Francisco: Harper & Row, 1985), p. 161.
12. *Ibid.*
13. Ted W. Engstrom and Edward R. Dayton, *The Christian Executive* (Waco, Texas: Word Books, 1979), p. 93.
14. *Ibid.*, p. 95.
15. *Ibid.*, p. 98.
16. *Ibid.*
17. *Ibid.*, p. 96.
18. Gordon MacDonald, *Ordering Your Private World* (Nashville, Tenn.: Oliver Nelson, 1984, 1985), p. 103.
19. J. Oswald Sanders, *Spiritual Leadership* (Chicago: Moody Press, 1967, 1980), p. 148.
20. *Ibid.*, pp. 151-152.

Chapter 13—Leadership—The Professional Dimension
1. Richard T. Pascale and Anthony G. Athos, *The Art of Japanese Management* (New York: Warner Books, 1981), p. 273.
2. John W. Gardner, *The Heart of the Matter* (Washington, D.C.: Independent Sector, 1986), p. 23.
3. *Ibid.*, pp. 23-24.
4. John W. Gardner, *The Moral Aspect of Leadership* (Washington, D.C.: Independent Sector, 1987), p. 4.
5. *Ibid.*
6. Michael Youssef, *The Leadership Style of Jesus* (Wheaton, Ill.: Victor Books, 1986), p. 163.

7. *Ibid.*
8. James L. Fisher, *Power of the Presidency* (New York: MacMillan Publishing Company, 1984), p. 45.
9. *Ibid.*, p. 46.
10. Pascale and Athos, *op. cit.*, p. 217.
11. James Carr, "Familiarity Breeds Contempt," *Pace*, December, 1986, p. 19.
12. Charette B. Kvernstoen, "The Secrets of Friendship," *Partnership*, January/February, 1987, p. 19.

Chapter 14—Loneliness and Leadership—The Spouse's View

1. Marylou Habecker, "The Dark Tarnish of Loneliness," *The United Brethren*, July, 1986, pp. 10-13.

Conclusion

1. John Stott, *Involvement: Social and Sexual Relationships in the Modern World, Vol. II* (Old Tappan, N.J.: Fleming H. Revell Company, 1984, 1985), p. 259.
2. *Ibid.*, pp. 258-259.
3. John White, *Excellence in Leadership* (Downers Grove, Ill.: Inter-Varsity Press, 1986), p. 88.
4. John W. Gardner, *The Moral Aspect of Leadership* (Washington, D.C.: Independent Sector, 1987), p. 9.
5. *Ibid.*
6. Rosabeth Moss Kanter, *The Change Masters* (New York: Simon & Schuster, 1983), p. 363.
7. *Ibid.*, pp. 363-364.
8. *Ibid.*, pp. 356-357.
9. White, *op. cit.*, pp. 88-89.
10. *Ibid.*, p. 41.
11. *Ibid.*, p. 89. See also, Donald V. Siebert, *The Ethical Executive* (New York: Simon & Schuster, 1984).